Joseph - Here's my Book
finally - I never got back
to you for reviewing it,
But Thanks for
Being available -

[signature]

Talking with Our Brothers

**CREATING AND SUSTAINING
A DYNAMIC MEN'S GROUP**

George M. Taylor

Talking With Our Brothers

Cover graphics by:
Marc Takaha, Takaha Graphics, Eureka, CA
Page design by:
Bill Ernst, Design Solutions, Mill Valley, CA

To order copies of Talking with Our Brothers:
Mail $11.50 per book ($9.50 plus $2 shipping
and taxes), and make checks out, to:
Men's Commmunity Publishing Project
P.O. Box 296, Fairfax, CA, 94930
Make check out to George Taylor.

DEDICATION

To a member of the finance committee, graphics review committee, editorial committee, visioning committee, and romance committee, my wife of 14 years, Debra Chamberlin Taylor, for her incredible support and for her thoughtful feedback.

And to my parents David Marr Taylor (deceased 1981) and my mother, Rosemary Quinn Taylor, for their support of my life as a writer and artist. Much appreciation for their open-mindedness.

TABLE OF CONTENTS

ACKNOWLEDGEMENTS

My first acknowledgement is to the thousands of men I have spent time with at retreats, groups and workshops, for their courage and their willingness to explore the pains of the past, so they can grow towards an optimistic future. And to the many men in my groups and retreats over the years, for their honesty.

My life has been irrevocably altered by the intelligence and dedication of the following teachers: Robert Bly, Michael Meade, James Hillman, Shepherd Bliss, Dominie Cappadonna, Stephen and Ondrea Levine, and Gay and Katie Hendricks. I am particularly grateful for the kindness and many acts of support of Jack Kornfield, meditation teacher.

Many colleagues in the San Francisco Bay Area and around the country generously offered me the fruits of their experience and wisdom, in personal conversations and by reviewing the manuscript. I include here Malidoma Some, Tony D'Aguano, Steve Sisgold, Michael Dennison, Chris Harding, John Guarnaschelli, Gordon Clay, Paul Boynton, Steve Downey, and Tom Daly. Special thanks to Lou Dangles for his efforts in developmental editing and in thinking through concepts of group dynamics which I labored to put into language.

Thanks to the Bay Area's Men's Counseling Guild, a unique group of men's work professionals who have been meeting for eight years to share knowledge of their professional work with men: Daniel Ellenberg, Bob Shelby, Gary Hoeber, Eric Grabow, Alan Ptashek, Russell Sutter, Steve Kessler, and Gerry Magaro.Special thanks to a former member of that group, my clinical supervisor with whom I shared many confusions and victories regarding clients in groups, Dr. Andrew Michaels.

My men's group has helped me with physical and emotional support: Grant Rudolph and Mark Shaffarman. Appreciation to John Dumitru and William McBride for fanatical copy-editing. Special thanks to Doug von Koss, teacher, colleague, friend and elder—you have given me so much inspiration to let out the artist I had trapped within.

I extend my great gratitude to my closest friends: Ane Takaha, Jo Alexander, Carolyn Hobbs, Pamela Polland, Stan and Devi Weisenberg, Valeta and Jeff Bruce, Ahria Wolf, Jay and Clare Wood, Michael Dennison—a great community of generous creative people known as the "fun hogs," many of whom I called for counsel and support in early 1995 when the creative stress and bliss were peaking.

Bill Ernst and Marc Takaha, fun hogs and extraordinary artists and men, have co-created this project with me, and I extend to them my gratitude for their skills, and for "being there."

I offer my thanks to the contributors to the community publication project which I describe in the introduction, who generously gave me permission to revise and republish the exercises which they submitted. (I list their names on the page of the activity they inspired.)

Introduction

One man who had been in my group for several years said, right after the moment of silence which usually begins our group meetings, "I felt so grateful as I sat in the quiet with you men. I rush around all the week doing things for others, accomplishing so much. I get so disconnected from myself.

"Coming to group is like going to church for me. I know that I can completely be myself." At this he started to cry. "I wish I could tell you what a profound relief this is. Just a profound relief. I try to practice what I learn here out in the world, telling the truth and being honest. Then I can come back for a reality check and for affirmation that this is indeed a worthy way of life. Thank you all so much." The group formed a circle around him and hugged him while he cried.

For ten years I have been meeting with men in large and small groups. We have sat together through pain, death, loss, joy, ecstasy, anger, and boredom because we want to break the chains of our gender roles which trap us into thinking that we only experience life in one or two narrowly restricted male models. We are dedicated to finding freedom together so we can express more of our innate compassion, power, and creativity. Mentors, colleagues of mine, and co-participants in groups have passed to me a torch, an inner knowing that affirms that men are good at heart, that we can heal ourselves and our brothers, and that this healing process is critically important for our world.

1

A powerful vehicle for this transformational work has been the small men's group. I speak as a man who has been transformed by this process, which has forced me and many men out of isolation and into community. It has required us to practice speaking a language rich in emotional nuance, so we can communicate our inner lives, and so our souls' movements toward healing can be made known.

We have had to acknowledge, through our tears and laughter, the depth of suffering and joy in our lives. In many cases, these depths of experience were complete secrets to us, so deep was our conditioning not to feel, and not to tell the truth. These experiments with small group dynamics have helped us find a safe place where we can transform the negative aspects of our male conditioning. This opportunity for growth has been a great gift to me personally. I wish to give back to my community the wealth of love, of creativity, and of insight which was so freely offered to me.

This book is a synthesis of my own experience as a participant in hundreds of men's events, and as a leader of workshops and small men's groups. I also come from a big family, where many of the dynamics described in this book were practiced everyday.

My experience and training have given me a deep appreciation for the mysteries of group process, which at its best can help us change old dysfunctional habits of communication and relationship, so we can express our passion and our pain more honestly and fully.

My own appreciation for men's groups and the men's movement continues to grow over time. I am proud to be a part of a communal, non-hierarchical process. This movement of men out of isolation and towards community has spawned thousands of men's groups around the country. Many of these support groups meet regularly two to four times a month; they ordinarily contain five to eight men, sometimes more. Other groups meet monthly, and have a larger attendance.

This book grew out of a project which began in the summer of 1992, when a group of volunteers organized a large multicultural community meeting for men in the San Francisco Bay Area. For this gathering we created a community publication which would allow men to exchange exercises which they had used in their small groups. The response to this project was overwhelming, and several volunteers and I put together a booklet of seventy-five activities.

The great response helped me realize that men wanted fresh ideas for exercises in their groups. And I knew that information about group dynamics which I had learned in graduate psychology classes, at workshops and retreats, and as a facilitator, could help groups get started and continue over time to help men open their hearts and touch their essential goodness. This book answers a simple question, "What information do small men's groups need to stay alive for a long period of time, so that members can change and grow?" I have tried to write for men who have found the desire for male community, but who may not have a background in group activity or in psychology. Group leaders with some training can also benefit from the stories, activities and practical applications of theory.

The book is an EASY-TO-USE guide to men's group activities that focuses on practical advice. I've covered several topics in some detail:

- **Why do men need men's groups?**
- **How do men's groups work?**
- **Why do men's groups fail?**
- **What types of men's groups are there?**
- **What types of exercises can men do in men's groups?**
- **How can a man, or a group of men, start a men's group?**
- **Men's resources: centers and publications**

My mentors, colleagues and friends in the men's community movement have been extraordinarily generous with me, and my life is forever changed because of their efforts. I offer this book back to that community, so that the chain of positive effects can continue. My hope is that men can find the deep connection with their essential goodness (which was such a part of my own healing) and share it with their friends, family and community.

Chapter 1

Guys Like Us Need Men's Groups

I first connected with the heart and soul of the then unnamed men's movement in the early 1980's. A friend had invited me to gatherings of men on the Northern California coast for two years, but family responsibilities (I mean, fear) prevented me from going. Finally, in the beautiful summer of 1984, Jay and I drove up together in his van, through the winding roads of Northern California, passing redwood groves and small winding streams. We stopped an hour from the retreat, took off all our clothes, and bathed in one of the roadside creeks, screaming at the cold water, and preparing ourselves for some mysterious initiation to come.

As we drove through the dappled shadows under the huge redwoods, I reflected on my interest in the all-men retreats. For over a year, I had heard that men from all walks of life, carpenters, doctors, plumbers, salesmen and artists, were gathering together. I was curious. I wanted to know who these men were and what they wanted to do together.

A deep need also drove me. I felt isolated—I needed friends and mentors. Life in late twentieth century America seemed too fast and confusing. Who could I talk to about my fears and hopes? Would I be able to find a community that wanted to find new, creative ways of being a man in our culture?

My mind was full of questions, and my body full of anxiety, as we turned away from the coast, and drove up deeper into the fog and redwoods behind Mendocino, California. When Jay and I pulled into the large campground, with its cabins and large central meeting hall, we were met by a short, dark-bearded, fierce character who stuck his head in the window of Jay's van and growled, "What do you want?"

I think he had been told to scare everyone who came in; his gruffness certainly worked on me. "Put your darn van over there, if you can fit it in. Sign in over here." Gesturing quickly to a row of dusty cars, the man was bossy, terse, and threatening, like the gatekeeper to some fairy tale land in which an odd adventure waited for me. The statuesque redwoods disappearing into the coastal fog overhead contributed to this other-worldly atmosphere.

We parked, unpacked, and gathered for dinner with about one hundred men. At dinner, we sat with men Jay had met at previous retreats. Their conversation nourished me. It was not about the latest car acquisition or job triumph. They spoke honestly about how being a man was changing, both in the culture, and inside their heads, and the joys and pains of that evolution. Jay said, "I need you guys. I need to be able to talk like this. A year is too long to not hear this kind of talk. Annie and I just had our second kid, and it's hard to stay connected to myself, let alone my wife and family. You guys remind me that the effort is well-worth it."

All around me I could see men, heads together, eating and talking. I heard a buzz of excited conversations, and by dessert, I felt part of something—a community, a tribe, who shared my needs to connect with and to inspire each other. After dinner, we pushed back the long tables and the benches. The night shadows grew long in the meeting hall which was surrounded by towering redwoods. We made a great circle of men in the hall. Arms entwined over shoulders, we chanted together and played drums. We danced around the great circle and raised up dust undisturbed for decades.

Then one after another, men walked or danced out into the middle of the circle and recited a poem about manhood or about the journey to consciousness. Some told stories of divorce, of job change, or of love. These men told their individual stories, but inside them I could hear all of our stories. I heard their confusion, their passion, their joys and sorrows. I heard men opening up to the full spectrum of life on our wild, beautiful suffering planet. The sound of their stories nourished my soul, which had been isolated and lacking in love.

I had longed for this feeling for a decade, and finally it pulsed, like deep chills, through my body that night as we danced and moved and talked to each other. After the long poetry circle, which broke up late in the night, I walked out into the foggy red-woods on my way back to my cabin.

In a deep way, I knew I had come home after a long solitary journey towards manhood. The men around me that night shared a dream of a different kind of masculine power and purpose, and they inspired me to pursue it with them.

That night under the moist redwoods, I wept tears of joy, of relief, of great joy, and the soft ground under the redwoods received my tears.

Later, after the retreat ended, with its pile of handmade arti-facts and drums loaded into cars, weeks and years went by as they will. I stayed in touch with men I met at that retreat. I found that the men who loved community and storytelling were just guys like me. We loved children, baseball, our friends, just like other guys. We were also men who loved to sweat and laugh and cry together, and be moved by the great tides of men's feelings. Family people, we wanted to heal ourselves so we could con-tribute more to our relationships.

When we came home from the retreats, we wanted to keep meeting, to tell more stories and heal the isolation that we felt. We came from all over the Bay Area, where I lived, to meet once a month, thirty to fifty strong, in a church gymnasium. We called ourselves the Golden Gate Men's Council. Gradually we created our own small groups, and these groups created other groups which met in churches, homes and recovery houses.

We were a poetic stream which joined with other streams of men who had been meeting since the early 1970's, when some of us with socio-political and economic concerns began writing about and meeting to discuss our gender roles. These men were supported and inspired by the women's movement. In the 1980's, the focus of men's groups broadened to include father's legal rights, recovery issues, and the spiritual life of men.

Now it is the '90s, an exciting time. Men and women have continued to ask deep questions about men's cultural roles, about our conditioning, and about the way we live, work and commu-nicate. The world of the '90s is a scary place sometimes, and we men have a deep need to find more ways to contribute to our own health, and the health of our families, communities and of the planet itself. Everywhere we go, we hear men and women crying out for more contact, for more community, for more compassion.

This has been a powerful decade for me personally. My own longing for community has been heard and received by many close male friends. Their support and truthtelling have helped me to heal some of my own shame, self-judgement, and lack of confidence. They have helped me through recovery from drug and alcohol abuse, and inspired me to more creativity and self-discovery.

With this group of friends and mentors, and an interlocking community of men with shared concerns across the country, I am participating in an important task: the rebuilding of our culture. We are operating with a strong sense of community, and we sense both our continuity with the communities of men from the past, and also our need to develop new ways of living and being in the world.

Small men's groups, like the ones I have been meeting with for a decade, are the yeast in this great cultural change. In these groups, men are creating pioneering ways of talking to each other, of being together, and of sharing our inner lives. We use simple but ancient tools: all-male gatherings, small circles of friends, storytelling, ritual, discussion and drama. The groups create communities where healing can happen; where men can dream, laugh, pray, and love; where we can practice talking truth to each other. Communities like these are the great antidotes for isolation, that one constant in the life of men in America, that one curse that so often leads to addiction, ill health, workaholism, and a host of other factors that cut short our lives and destroy our happiness and self esteem.

This book is a resource so that these men's groups can grow and flourish. I offer it as my contribution to this healing community. It synthesizes my own experience in many group settings, and it is a testimony to the great creativity that is moving through so many men as we seek to grow and change.

CHAPTER 2

THE BENEFITS OF MEN'S GROUPS

Much of the effect of the negative conditioning which men receive in our intensive maculine training programs could be summarized in one word: isolation—isolation from our partners, from our families, from our communities, as well as from our spiritual lives and our hopes and passions.

Fortunately, consistent participation in a men's group works a spell of magic on our tendency to isolate. This process begins when men make the commitment to regularly attend group meetings, and it continues for as long as cohesion and trust exists between the members. I have seen men three and four years into a small group together still shedding layers of armoring and mistrust to reveal deep wounds and truths.

Several years ago one of my men's groups went on an overnight camping trip. We told each other our life histories. Our goal was to hear and see each other in newer, deeper ways. Many tears were shed when men told parts of their stories that they had not told to other men before, and felt the group honor their private lives and secrets.

Such a deepening experience sends a great ripple through a group; men's needs for deep intimacy are touched, as well as their fears of being hurt. This dual result showed itself in the group a few weeks later. A man named Fred expressed to the group his need for support, and how little empathy he felt from the other men.

His way of communicating his disappointment and anger was oblique. He said, "It's curious to me that you guys don't walk your talk. I wonder what that is about. No one has called me, even though I put out strongly last week that I was hurting, with my business being so slow and the bills piling up. Are we trying to connect only here in this room or do we try to carry this out into the world?"

Immediately, another man said, "Why do I feel guilty when I hear your question?"

Fred responded quickly, "I'm just asking a question. I'm not blaming." I looked around the group and could tell that not everyone agreed with him. Fred had put his finger on an important topic which comes up over and over in men's groups; How do we carry our experiments in truthtelling out into the world? I have taken part in many discussions about the difference between telling the truth in your group about how someone's comments affect you, and telling your supervisor on the job the same thing.

But Fred was also expressing his disappointment indirectly. He was not able that night to talk honestly about his deeper feelings, and the group ended on a discordant, anxious note. But by the next meeting, Fred was more vulnerable. He said, "I realized in the last week that I was trying to express my own disappointment. I feel so needy now, with my business problems, and it's hard to admit that. It was easier to be angry with you for not meeting my needs. And of course, that's a projection from my father, who so rarely could listen to me."

The group and I relaxed as Fred revealed his inner experience. As other men talked about the same need for nurturing and support, we healed the anxious disconnected feeling from the week before. We had practiced a new way to resolve conflict—through truthtelling and forgiveness—and felt the reward for that courageous action.

Fred's insight into his own process inspired me, and the interchange also helped me to see just how deep our conditioning is. This group had been intact for three years at this point, and members still carried their anger as a protective shield. The good news is that members could see and feel their protectiveness—how they reacted to Fred's anger with guilt, and with anger of their own. Bringing awareness and intention to such feelings and patterns of reaction begins the process of change, of warming up those numb, defended parts of ourselves so we can make better choices when we respond to people.

This vignette is an example of one of the five ways (at least) that groups help support human growth and awareness.

1. Groups automatically recreate old emotional patterns of relationship and communication which we learned from our parents and families. As in the example with Fred, group participants can see these patterns clearly, and this witnessing allows for insight and change.

2. Men's groups help participants to break down isolation, which makes us think that our feelings and experiences are unique to ourselves. In dialogue with our brothers, we see that we react and think much like other men. Many of our dysfunctional behaviors are locked into place in our psyche because we are in denial that they actually happen. Hearing others' experience normalizes our inner process, and this awareness allows change to occur. We can let go of our shame that we are not perfect, that we don't have all the answers, and speak more freely from our own experience.

One man at a workshop I led several years ago raised the question of sexual dysfunction between him and his wife. He said that generally he had great sex with his partner, but maybe a third of the time he prematurely ejaculated, and then his wife became angry. He then felt shame and powerlessness.

Participants in the workshop talked about this topic for a long time. Obviously, he had hit a vein of interest, and each man said that he had had experiences of impotence or premature ejaculation. The sharing ranged all the way from practical suggestions about sexual technique to questions about communication between him and his wife.

I asked about his anger and how he expressed it, and he admitted that passive-aggressive behavior was a trait of his. After the long dialogue, the man said, "I never knew that my problem was so common, and I really appreciate the openness of other men to educate me. I feel a lot better about my plight, and I feel hopeful that I can learn to be more direct with my anger."

3. Men can learn to express more of our inner lives and truths. We have been pressured by other men since we were born to act "manly." The pressure is relentless and intense, and the effectiveness of this training program is shown in the universality

of the results: so many of us act like the John Wayne hero—"I can solve it myself, ma'am."

The hero image occupies a place of tremendous importance in men's psyches, and has inspired men to great acts of courage and creativity. The shadow side of the image exerts a tremendous cost: often the hero cannot ask for help, and he cannot be less than perfect.

A group helps us find a place and a set of relationships where we can practice being more fully ourselves, where we don't have to adjust our behavior and our conversations to fit others' needs and demands. In groups, men can test these new behaviors and receive honest feedback from others about them.

This new behavior was demonstrated by Ted, a man who had been in my group for several years (the same vignette I used in the Introduction). He said, right after the moment of silence which usually begins our group meetings, "I felt so grateful as I sat in the quiet with you men. I rush around all the week doing things for others, accomplishing so much. I get so disconnected from myself.

This night is like going to church for me. I know that I can completely be myself." At this, he started to cry. "I wish I could tell you what a relief it is. I try to practice what I learn here, telling the truth and being honest, then I can come back here for a reality check and for affirmation that this is indeed a worthy way of life. Thank you all so much."

The group formed a circle around him and hugged him while he cried. And I was deeply moved when I realized that this man, Ted, was creating a new model of being a hero—a hero who uses the support of his community to change, and to wage a deep struggle against old forms of behavior

4. Groups help men to feel intimate with others. This process connects us with our own needs, our hurts, and our own desires, and it makes it easier for us to feel and connect with others. Many men need practice being close to others and talking honestly about their warm loving feelings.

In groups, I create activities which allow men to talk directly to each other. (Some of these are in this book.) In these safe meetings, men often express deep feelings of respect or love for each

12

other. And oftentimes I notice that the man being addressed looks away, or makes a quick quip.

We are so unused to being loved. I'll try to slow that moment down and say, "Wait a minute, let's take a breath and feel what's really going on here." Then the kind feeling lingers between the two men, and they can enjoy it together.

5. A ritual group helps men to connect with a spiritual feeling which many of us have wanted, but have been unable to find in current churches. Through chanting, meditating, or dancing together, men can nourish an ancient desire to experience religious connection, and this connection heals some of our isolation and anxiety.

For example, in our groups, we generally ritualize the end of each year. This year, at the winter solstice, I turned out all the lights when the group members arrived, and set eight candles on the floor in the darkness. I asked the men one by one to light a candle and express their thoughts about the year gone by and the year to come.

When we were done, one man said, "It feels so great to be in the dark together and to honor the shortness of the days. Slowing down is how I feel, I want to be home with my family and be warm. I rush around so much trying to get things done. I forget that I have a body and a heart. What a great ritual."

These are only some of the benefits which accumulate to members of men's groups. Group work is a powerful antidote to isolation, because it commits us to interactions over time. We learn new skills of communication and conflict resolution, and we create a healing community together. This learning and creating has profound effects on us, our families and our communities.

CHAPTER 3

WHY GROUPS FAIL

COMMON PATTERNS IN
GROUP BEHAVIOR

At least six predictable patterns of behavior and communication will emerge in a group. If the members let these patterns unfold without attention, then they will get stuck in certain roles and ways of communicating. The feeling of dynamic growth and expectancy that marks the beginning of a group can disappear, and the group is likely to fragment, because members will begin to feel distant from each other.

These patterns are not good or bad, they happen automatically, like gravity. If the group is willing to pay attention to them, this awareness can lead to understanding of how we communicate, both within the group and outside, and can help enormously in our relationships.

Two of the patterns involve how the members create the group: Commitment and Leadership. The four other patterns are personal or psychological issues which will emerge as men meet with each other: Creating and Avoiding Intimacy; Family Patterns; Dominance; and Truthtelling vs. Blaming

General questions follow each description. These questions can lead to useful activities if group members plug them into the discussion format in Chapter 7.

CREATING THE GROUP

Commitment

This is a question of involvement: Are group members committed to the process? Are agreements about commitment, attendance, and promptness clear enough so that men can keep them? Laxness about creating the container of the group is a statement of intention; it says something like, "I want an escape valve so I don't really have to be here."

If attendance becomes a consistent problem for a man, often he is showing his dissatisfaction for the group in the only way he knows how. Of course, men need to stay current with other members if their commitment level changes. It is easy to make the absent member the scapegoat for ambivalence that other members may be feeling, but do not know how to talk about. It is important to remember that the real commitment is for group members to be present and willing to invest themselves, their truth, and their vulnerability into the group.

Key Questions

1. *Are the agreements about when and where the group meets clear? Do the group members come on time and consistently? Do members expect a call when someone is going to miss a meeting?*

2. *Do group members feel free to talk about their own or others' lateness or missed meetings? What emotional reactions do these misses trigger in other members? How are these reactions familiar from previous relationships?*

3. *Do the members come ready to be present, or are they affected by their working pace, or drugs like alcohol or coffee?*

Leadership

Who is going to run the group, and how will this be decided? How will group decisions be made? Questions like these inevitably arise when men get together to create something. Men have found great inspiration and energy with good leaders, and they have been wounded and abused by bad ones. This history will be present in a group, especially at the beginning, as the members begin to develop some trust.

John Guarnaschelli, who has put together dozens of men's groups through his organization "On the Common Ground" in New York City, has suggested to me that this is the one hurdle that his groups struggle with the most. Men sometimes launch into group work together without handling this single fundamental issue: how will the members decide where to meet, when to meet, and most importantly, how will they meet? The failure to create a common agreement means that some men will unconsciously take power, and others will give it up. Unspoken resentments will build, until someone has the courage to tell the truth, or until the group fragments.

Key Questions

1. *What kind of leader do I want for this group? Do I want to be the only leader? Will I give my respect to another leader? Do I want leadership to rotate, or rest with one individual?*

2. *What kinds of issues do I have around leadership? Do I want to control and manage, or do I sit back and criticize? How do I react when I am being lead or controlled and I don't like it?*

3. *Am I willing to make leadership a topic of the group? Am I willing to speak honestly about my needs when the leaders do not appear to be taking them into account?*

PERSONAL DYNAMICS

About two years ago, my leaderless group was interviewing a new man. We asked him about his history with men's work and men's groups, and he droned on for several minutes about the history of feminism and how men had been battered by the media. I felt the rest of us shifting and getting nervous, and finally one of the members, John, interrupted him and said, "You know, I checked out about five minutes ago. What are you really talking about?"

Tim, the man being interviewed, was angry at first. "Hey, I just met you an hour ago. Give me a chance..." He took a deep breath. "You sound frustrated with me. I understand that. I'm experiencing this fluttery feeling in my belly, and I know I'm anxious. I really want you guys to like me. I'm hellbent on trying to impress you with how sensitive I am." He laughed. "Of course, I'm not trying to be sensitive and vulnerable, I'm trying to impress. Quite a different thing."

When Tim identified his inner experience, I felt the group open to him. His self-exposure helped John to become vulnerable too, and he said, "What I think happens for me is two things. First I want to know you, and I can't feel anything, untill the last few minutes. And second, my father used to have these heart to

17

heart talks with me, but he'd just ramble on and never ask me what I wanted to say. They were head to head talks, and I used to sit there getting more and more impatient. That's what I felt listening to you."

There are many important group dynamics present in this short example. First, Tim's entry into the group showed him a habit he had about keeping distance from people, and the group gave him immediate feedback about it. And John's reaction told us about his relationship with his father, and how his family dynamics were brought up by Tim's check-in.

Group life is so rich, because it is constantly revealing such intimate details. Here are the four basic patterns of personal dynamics which groups will flush up out of the members.

Creating and Avoiding Intimacy

Everything that happens within a group either promotes intimacy or distance. Each group member uses methods to accomplish these two tasks which are personal to his own history of relationship.

The group level of intimacy must be a topic that men can discuss honestly with each other. Otherwise members will eventually reach a plateau of intimacy, and they will experience restlessness or boredom.

Key Questions

1. *When I want to create intimacy, how do I speak? What do I say? What do I talk about? How does my voice sound? When I am scared or vulnerable, what do I talk about?*

2. *When I want to create distance, how do I speak? What do I say? What do I want to talk about?*

3. *Am I attentive to the group, to different members of the group when they speak? Do I connect better with certain members of the group than with others? Why? What do these connections say about my own history? What kind of men do I like and dislike?*

4. *When I feel intimate with men, what feelings come up inside me? Openness, embarrassment, fear, love, homophobia? What do I actually do when I feel close to men?*

Family Patterns

Group members immediately begin to relate to others in ways which they learned in their family, community, and culture. Each member will tend to take a role similar to his role in his family: elder son, scapegoat, victim, youngest son, critic, philosopher, caretaker, etc.

In an atmosphere of trust and support, these old patterns can be made conscious. The holdover feelings from other times, can be seen, recognized, and changed. Members can learn to stop acting unconsciously and reactively, and learn to broaden their potential responses to people and the world.

Key Questions

1. *What role did I have in my original family? What did my parents expect me to act like? How is my behavior within the group like my family role?*

2. *When I sit in the group, how old do I feel? How old do I feel in relation to the other men? Do I feel more intelligent, aware, or involved? How is this a familiar feeling?*

3. *What behaviors are elicited from me which are unique to this configuration of men? Do I get quieter than usual or anxious? Do I interrupt or sit passively?*

Male Patterns of Dominance

Some men take up room in conversations even when they have nothing to say. In a group, this behavior is hard to conceal. Other group members will react to being dominated or controlled: they become angry, mute, sarcastic, or passive-aggressive. Oftentimes both the control and the reactions come out in quick, supposedly humorous comments.

Key Questions

1. *Who takes up the most speaking time in the group? What kind of speaking is he doing: generalizing, storytelling, blaming, theorizing?*

2. *What feelings do other group members have when they don't get a chance to speak to the group?*

3. *How do group members behave when they are uncomfortable with the speaker? Do they sulk, interrupt, space out,*

make sarcastic remarks? What do they really want to say?

4. *How were we trained in our families as group members: to take up time, to be quiet, to speak when spoken to? How do these training patterns show up in our group?*

Truthtelling vs. Blaming

Many men have been trained to control their feelings and situations by blaming and criticizing others. This way of communicating creates distance between people, rather than closeness. It also limits self-awareness which can develop as members learn to look inward at their own reactivity. Often as members get closer, their defensive behaviors are activated. They haul out their inner gunslinger for protection and begin blazing away. A group will trigger and magnify these defended forms of communication, and if there is too much blaming and anger, the group will not feel safe.

Group members also have an opportunity to practice other, healthier forms of communication and conflict resolution. One basic method to practice is for group members to tell the truth about their own experience rather than blaming the other member for reactions or judgements. Most of the time when group members react deeply to each other, it's because some emotional memory has been triggered. For example, a member may have a special charge when someone comes late to the meeting because his father was often late and disappointed him.

Truthtelling opens members up to their own experience and is an essential skill to learn in groups. As in the example above, when Tim could identify his own inner experience of anxiety, he invited the whole group into an experience of intimacy. When we blast away, criticize, and blame, we push others away.

Key Questions

1. *When I am in a conflict, do I usually describe my experience or the other person's? Do I attack, blame, or criticize?*

2. *Do I even know what my inner experience of anger or hurt feels like? What are the bodily sensations of my emotions?*

3. *What kind of communications do I need to make to create resolution after conflict? What kind of communications creates more conflict?*

4. *Am I willing to explore my own emotional history, and take the focus off the other man, when I am in conflict?*

Conclusion

Any of these important topics can be turned into an activity simply by following the model for a discussion I suggest in Chapter 7, and substituting the questions which I have given here.

CHAPTER 4

TWO TYPES OF GROUPS
PERMANENT OR
ROTATING LEADERSHIP

Over the last twenty years two different types of men's groups have evolved: groups with a trained leader who organizes the night's activities, and groups with a rotating leader chosen from among the members. An example might help clarify some important differences between these two types of groups.

My unfacilitated group had been meeting for several years, and we had achieved a high level of cohesion and trust. At one of our meetings, Tom spoke about a business opportunity and its importance for his self esteem and his family finances. He spoke softly and vulnerably. "This opportunity gives me a chance for a professional recognition which I have wanted for many years, and a chance for acknowledgement from my wife as family provider...You guys know what stress I have been under about that."

John, another group member, was disturbed by this story and interrupted him to say, "That's bullshit. Your hair-brained business plans never work..."

A stunned silence filled the room. Tom took a deep breath and said, "What are you trying to tell me? I'm pissed that you would interrupt me to tell me something that is so critical and uncaring..."

Immediately John apologized. "You're right, you're right. Let's go on with your story..." So Tom continued.

As someone with training in group process, I felt frustrated at that moment. The personal dynamic between the two men and the undercurrent of feeling in John fascinated me. A trained group facilitator would have intervened to ask John what was triggered in him when he listened to Tom. The angry outburst looked like the expression of jealousy or of hurt, which John might have benefitted from talking about in the moment.

At the end of the meeting, in our closing circle, John had a forced smile on his face. His anger and subsequent embarrassment hadn't gone away. The two men talked by phone about the episode during the week, and John revealed that he felt trapped by his own family role as the breadwinner.

When he heard about Tom's business success, and his breaking free of work he didn't want to do, his upset about his own life work burst out of him. John reported this phone call to us and he again apologized for the unclear, blaming way his own feelings had come out at Tom. John and Tom both said that they felt closer after their phone call.

It's hard to judge which route of exploration is more beneficial—groups with a permanent leader or with rotating leaders within the group. If these two men hadn't felt the trust which grows from a long relationship, the deep feelings involved may never have surfaced without a facilitator to inquire into them. The bonding within the group could have suffered a permanent subtle break. (This residue of old feelings is a primary contributing factor which causes groups to disintegrate. See Chapter 9 for more information.)

There's no right answer. Some men want a group with a leader who sets the ground rules and creates the emotional atmosphere for other men to do their work in. Other men want a group in which leadership rotates from week to week, and each member is responsible for creating activities and observing group process.

Men choose different types of groups based on many factors:

- Availability of groups with trained leaders;
- Personal interest in leadership and in creating activities;
- Background in men's events;
- Cost factors (facilitatation costs $15 to $40 per session);
- The desire for the safety a leader can create;
- The desire to explore group life without leaders.

These are subtle topics to evaluate, and often your decision will simply come down to the availablility of different types of groups in your area.

GROUPS WITH REGULAR LEADERS

Advantages

A regular, trained leader does many tasks for the group; he finds members and interviews them, schedules and presents activities, and defines the types of communication that he expects. As an observer and facilitator, he holds the group safety in his hands.

A regular leader creates the vision of how the group operates. He holds the image of how transformation and how group process work. For example, in my group I try to make the vision as clear as possible. When men join, I ask them to tell the truth at all times, to be responsible for their own feelings, and not to blame. Of course, these high standards are not always possible, but they provide important guidelines for the men to conform to. I also have clear requirements about payment, promptness, and absences. These agreements help create an environment in which members can trust each other and in which they can grow in intimacy and self-responsibility over time.

As my example shows, group leaders usually will call attention to intergroup process, to the subtle comments and interactions in which group members reveal interpersonal information. This level of in-the-moment truthtelling may be scary and exciting to group members. But over my years in group work, I have seen that the immediacy of feelings and reactions is the lifeblood of the group. If groups members can find a way, either with a leader or without, to tell the truth about how they are doing, men can transform their self-image and their communication skills. A good leader will train his members how to listen carefully to conversations, how to detect when a lot of feeling is present, how to ask about it, and how to spot deflections and misstatements which evade emotional depth.

A leader has authority ceded to him by the group. This process recreates a family system with a father in charge and brothers of equal rank. The men present agree to a specific hierarchy, in which someone is appointed to moderate conflicts and preserve the safety of members under attack. Because of the leader's unique position within the group, eventually the members will begin to develop strong feelings about him. This development, called "transference," is an important part of group process. Exploring issues of transference helps group members gain insight into, and transform relationships with, fathers, mentors, and other elders.

For example, several years ago, Frank, a man in a group I was leading, wanted to develop a program for business men to go into the wilderness together. He was going through a major career transition, trying to create a new business from the ground floor up. Because of my experience starting workshop programs, he talked about asking me to help him, but he never followed through.

Then finally he started off one meeting by looking at me and saying, "I'm really mad at you. I kept wanting you to reach out to me to ask me, to help me with my project. I'm really pissed..."

I could feel my face flush and my blood racing to defend myself, but I also knew that Frank had showed the group an important pattern in his life, so I encouraged him to keep talking and to be as mad as he wanted to be at me. He said, "I'm so pissed off. You're so understanding, but you don't reach out to me." His voice was getting louder and louder, and his accusations went on and on.

Then his voice cracked a little. "You know, this is my pattern. I don't think you really want to help, so I don't ask. Then I can become the perfect victim. I see that. I see that and I want to heal it...Thanks for hanging in with me..." He reached over and gave me a hug, and I felt a huge wave of relief go through both of us. My holding the emotional ground in this interaction gave him a chance to go all the way through his feelings to acceptance and peacefulness.

Disadvantages to Group Leadership

If the leader cannot highlight the subtle but ongoing group dynamics, the group will eventually stagnate. Members will feel uneasy, as if there is something that needs to be said but no one is sure what. Men will simply not feel safe. They will not risk the types of injuries which we have received in the past: shaming, abuse, or disempowerment.

A good leader will also train members to observe their own and other's feelings and reactions, and to talk about them with sympathy. An inexperienced leader can subtly disempower group members, so he is the only one exerting leadership or making interventions in group process. Then men don't get this essential training.

When I began facilitating groups, I thought that I had to do a lot in the group: prepare complex exercises and intervene brilliantly and often. Of course, I wanted to give myself a feeling of higher self esteem through my work, and I thought this meant I had to be an active leader. In my insecurity, I over-controlled, and there was less room for members to participate and to be creative.

As the years have gone by, I find myself sharing leadership more easily and collaborating with my groups in creating activities. As I give up more control, men have more room to be creative and to say what they want. We have had some tremendous fun co-creating rituals for fathers and sons and planning backpack trips together.

Sharing power is a difficult process for anyone, but if the group leader holds on too much, the men will eventually become frustrated. The group will either break out in unexplained anger, or men will simply stop coming.

Key Questions to Ask a Group Leader

1. *What is your vision of the group? Why are you leading a men's group?*

2. *How long have you been leading groups?*

3. *What happens when new men join the group? Does the group decide, or you?*

4. *How are the new men assimilated?*

5. *Do groups focus on interactive work between men inside the group or on check-in (men reporting on their life between group meetings) or on work between client and leader?*

6. *How is conflict handled?*

7. *Are group members allowed to comment on their relationship with the leader?*

8. *What happens when they do? How are they received?*

9. *What happens when group members get mad?*

10. *Do they have permission to go deeply into their emotions?*

11. *Can you give examples of this?*

GROUPS WITH ROTATING LEADERSHIP

Advantages

In groups with rotating leadership, members take more responsibility for the group structure and activities. They create the group vision. In this process, they have to be creative. These opportunities give members practice so they can use these skills in other settings. Within the group setting, they also get clear feedback about their leadership skills and their creativity.

Many leaderless groups do have structures for creating direct dialogue between men. For men in other types of group, a lack of focus on group process and on interactive dialogue may be a positive advantage. When I described some of the direct confrontational dialogues that we have had in our small group to Marty, a friend in a different group, he said, "Wow, our group isn't so interactive. We decided to focus on a supportive, nurturing, listening atmosphere for our meetings, and in many ways we have succeeded. I need the feeling that these guys love me and want to hear from me, no matter what I express."

We were sitting out on my deck watching the California fog roll over the hills across our little valley, and Marty put down his tea. He looked out over the big grey clouds and a big tear rolled out of his eyes. He took off his thick glasses and said. "All my life, since I was on the farm with my dad, I wanted someone to say, 'You're okay, Marty, you're okay.' I feel that in my group so intensely. They don't need me to bring a thousand bales of hay to be good..."

I realized then that many models of group work will benefit men. This form of leaderless group, focusing on support, can give members an acknowledgement that we may have longed for from our parents or elders and never received.

Disadvantages

Lack of comments on process may mean that subtle communication dynamics are not discussed. When men in the group are peers, no one is empowered necessarily to intervene or to interrupt long monologues. Members may often be reluctant to comment on each other directly.

Furthermore, if no one asks direct questions to a man who is on the edge of some important realization or feeling, he may not access this information as quickly as he could with a leader.

In leaderless groups, decision-making can be long and laborious, especially if men's need for control or their competitiveness is triggered, and the group doesn't have a way to explore these deep issues.

Lastly, men may shy away from conflict without the safety of a leader present, and go numb and become distant in the group. Conversely, men may feel anxious and uncentered, and lash out at each other as a safety mechanism. These discordant emotions can be a challenge if no one is trained in facilitating expression of them in a self-responsible way.

Conclusion

Much of the information in this book is intended to give concepts, tools, and activities to help men deal with the subtle issues raised by leaderless groups.

CHAPTER 5

TYPES OF EXERCISES

DISCUSSIONS, CREATIVE ARTS PROCESSES AND RITUALS

Most group activities divide into three main groups: discussion exercises which give men a forum to speak about their concerns, questions, and desires; creative arts processes which ask men to play and to move together, and to pay attention to what happens when we do; and rituals which are traditional, sacred activities—chanting, dancing, drumming, meditating—which many men have adapted to meet current needs.

Men's groups use any mix of these exercises: some groups stick to discussion in all their meetings, some use only ritual. Others combine and recombine activities depending on which group member is leading that week. Men ask me, "Which type of exercises should our group do first? When should we start with a ritual?" I give some thoughts on these questions in this chapter, but more and more I realize that I have to give these questions back to the group, and let them decide. This process models consensus building and cooperation.

I describe four developmental stages that groups go through: Beginning the Group; Going Deeper; Plateaus and Problems; and Going Deeper Again.

In the beginning stage of the group, members should focus on discussion activities, which orient the group to its purpose, and which help introduce members to each other. Consequently in Chapter 7, I list several important discussion topics on these themes, and I add some simple rituals for beginning and ending the meetings.

In the next three chapters, corresponding to the other developmental stages, I include all three types of exercises. Chapter 8 describes the exciting second stage of a group, when bonding is occurring and men feel great about meeting. In Chapter 9, I list many interactive discussion activities which help men break through to new levels of truthtelling and intimacy, the third stage of the group. Often it takes several meetings (or several months) before the group has created enough trust for the men to be ready for direct, honest dialogue.

I save some of the evocative ritual and creative arts activities for Chapter 10, the fourth stage of the group, because often these activities take some experience in ritual-making or in creative arts processes. These are the broadest of guidelines. Generally men will do exercises that they have some experience with (through other groups, workshops, etc.), or that they read about. They will learn what works in their group only by trying, by discussing their attempts with fellow members, and by learning from failures, hopefully with some humor.

Discussion Exercises

Secrets men have carried for decades are often revealed and discussed within groups. Discussion exercises provide oportunities for men to share a huge body of communal experience and wisdom that we usually don't get to talk about on topics like: how does our penis work; how do we handle the stress of changing jobs; how do we work with death in the family; how does our sexuality change as we age. Many of us are trained to pretend we have all the answers.

Many times in groups I have heard men say, "Oh that happens for you too? I thought I was the only one..." Our silence keeps us wondering if we are the only ones with certain very normal experiences. Once I was facilitating a group of men interested in relationship, and the topic was power. One man said, "All my life I have shied away from power. My father was very violent, especially when anyone disagreed with him. Now my wife tells me over and over, '...you've got to make some decisions, you've got to take charge of your life.' I know she's right, but it's so hard to change my ways. I can feel a change coming, but I'm in a muddle. Exerting my own power is so scary. I'm not used to imposing my will on the world, or asking people for what I need. I used to get clobbered when I did that."

I could see his throat working, holding back a sob, so I asked, "Peter, what do you think you have lost by..." He interrupted me and started to cry, "Only myself, only my own dreams and hopes." A man in the group held him until he stopped crying.

Then other group members chimed in about how power was hard for them to express too. One said, "I grew up with a model that only one person could have power at a time. Now I'm fighting with my wife and I see how it's the same thing. Only one person gets their way, and if it isn't me, I brood for days. This causes so much pain for me and my wife, and I can see my kids' reactions too. I'm committed to finding a new way of sharing power so that others could be powerful too." Men's heads nodded, and gradually Peter looked up and looked around.

I could see in his expression a new resolve to wrestle with this power issue, and to find a way to be powerful in a compassionate loving way, not in the old model he had learned.

Topics such as this one, as well as many presented in this book, can serve as models for hundreds of discussions between men. These discussions usually focus on men's personal experiences. Even when group members discuss a book or a tape, the key to engaged conversations is personalizing the material. I have given many tips on how to do this in the descriptions of the activities.

Creative Arts Processes

Men sit together in groups to share truth and to learn to love better. For some men this process includes creating and moving together in new ways. We sense that there is more life and excitement inside of us, and we want to find ways to let these inner feelings and strengths out. We also learn that the numbness we experience has a physical component. If we can activate our bodies and our emotions, we can reclaim our aliveness.

In response to these needs, men's groups are developing different creative arts exercises, drawing on other healing movements. For example, men in one branch of the men's movement are sharing a rebirth of the love of poetry, story, and drama. We are exploring the roots of sacred drama, song, and meditation by creating exercises which explore these ancient arts. These activities draw on the work of Carl Jung with active imagination.

Specialists in family therapy and in recovery work have created activities which help us to express secret characters who live within us. Oftentimes men in groups act out creative episodes

33

from stories they have written or heard, or from dreams. Or we role play stories from our childhood which still haunt us in some way. In these role plays, we can release old emotional energy and feel freer and more alive.

The creative arts activities I have outlined in the book ask group members to move and talk and play in new ways, healing ways, and to be conscious of how we are feeling while we are creating together. We learn that creativity is fun, that life flows through the body and is good, and that transformation can be humorous and pleasurable.

Many movement activities in the book ask us to act out characters, to state visions or intentions, or to express ourselves honestly with our bodies. Men can practice observing each other closely when we perform these activities. Often stiffness in the body is a primary way for us to hold feelings out of consciousness. Group members should ask permission to give feedback, and then comment if they see signals like: tight jaws or hands, movement in the throat, held-in breath, eyes glancing down or away, or incompleted movements. You can ask the man at these times to breathe in deeper, to exaggerate his movements, and to explore what might lie under these body cues.

Rituals

Our twentieth century culture is marked by a loss of connection to sacred ceremonies. Many of us are not aware that most other human cultures had a defined set of rituals to express their relationship to the divine. Many men still feel a great human need to acknowledge that something mysterious and large operates in the universe.

In men's communities, we are creatively taking apart old rituals and ceremonies and refashioning them for this current need. We are using the same basic components: silence, prayer, meditation, rhythm, song, and movement. These rituals seem more specific and more intentional than the ones I experienced as a young Catholic.

We create rituals which connect us to the vast elemental forces and components of the universe: light, dark, earth, air, fire, water, and life itself. We know we live on a fragile ball of matter that circles the sun, and that our lives belong to these great circles of planet, galaxy and star. Ceremonies that are thousands of years old cannot always express the depth with which we honor and love our particular place in the cosmos.

These new rituals provide great opportunity for sacred connections, but they are challenging for both their creators and for the participants. The challenge within a ritual is to keep everyone involved; issues of power, creativity, and dominance spring up whenever men try new projects together. Why should ceremony creation be any different?

I remember one ritual failure I experienced back in the early days of the Golden Gate Men's Council. We used to let anyone who wanted to lead our monthly meeting. A fellow named Mark, who was new to the group, volunteered to lead us in a ritual in the hills of Marin County, just north of San Francisco. It was late summer, with warm days and a warm ocean.

He decided that we would take a three mile hike to a secluded cove on a steep path that I knew well. He wanted us to bring drums and lunch. Knowing how rugged the oceanside cliffs were, I brought a little shaker, but some guys showed up with their huge congas slung over their shoulders, not knowing how far they would be carrying them.

At the beginning of the hike, we made the now-traditional circle, and chanted some chants that no one knew, including one to Norwegian gods that no one had any connection with, "Thor, Wodan, Loki..." Since Loki was the trickster god, we said his name in a high pitched giggle. The chant went on and on, with Mark finally being the only singer. By then there was much grumbling around the circle. Men couldn't connect with the images and sounds of this chant. As for me, looking back on the day, I realized that I would never invoke a trickster god before a long hike into the wilds.

We broke up the circle and walked up a fire road towards the beautiful California rolling hills. Near a creek bed, we took the first of two roads that went off to the right. I was concerned, because I knew that the second road led to our destination, but I let go, and decided that Mark must have scouted another way. About two hours later, the fire road had petered out high in the foggy hills into a narrow deer trail, the conga drum carriers were nearing exhaustion, and we were totally lost, miles from Pirates

Cove, our intended destination. It was obviously too late for me to say, "By the way, I know which is the right road." I would have been buried under a pile of heavy congas and set ablaze.

After another couple of hours, we stumbled back down to the main fire road and walked out to the public beach, which by now was deserted, since a tremendous breeze had sprung up. The water temperature had fallen with the sun. Mark insisted on going ahead with his original plan. Guys were cooling off and sweat-stained in the cold wind. Then he formed us into a long line and said, "Okay, together like brothers we walk into the ocean for a rebirth."

Most of the group rebelled, yelling, "Are you out of your mind? First you get us lost, cold, freezing, soaking wet, hungry and tired, and now you want us to go into the ocean?" By this time it was pitch black, and I had the only flashlight. Half of the group wanted to throw Mark into the ocean and hold him under as a sacrifice to Loki for our foolishness in trusting him.

I describe this ritual in such detail because it violates three of the five main rules I have learned about creating ceremonial events with men.

1. Keep ritual simple. If ritual leaders are imposing meaning and significance on activities or objects, they can activate many power and control issues in the participants that will make it hard for them to connect with the sacred. Complex processes and images can divert us from simple religious feelings and expressions.

2. Group members should be encouraged to cooperate in the ritual creation. The more people in the group who have helped create the ceremony, the better it will go. Often group leaders make sure the group is in agreement as it moves from step to step, by asking participants if it is okay to go on. This consensus building helps men to join their wills and their hearts together.

3. Often we do not give ritual making the time and attention it deserves. An hour of chanting or drumming or dancing can have a far more profound effect on the psyche than just ten minutes.

4. Leaders should walk through the whole ritual step by step, before the group meets, to see where men will stand, sit, and move, and how ritual items will be utilized.

5. Everything in a group takes twice as long as the time planned for it. This is especially true with a ritual.

CHAPTER 6

STARTING A GROUP

When we start our own men's group, we are responding to a deep need for contact, for male wisdom, for brotherhood. All of our conditioning which says that we should remain isolated rises up in our face like some great demon. Also, subtle childhood messages, like "I can't get what I want," or "No one really wants to be my friend," are activated by acting on this desire.

So take a deep breath and begin.

In this chapter I've laid out a road map through this difficult and adventure-filled territory of the psyche, where our needs are in conflict with our fears and insecurities. I've described some lessons I've learned from my own experience starting and joining many different groups, including: Personal Issues in Starting a Group; Locating Men; Maintaining the Vision. Chapter 7 presents activities which will help you in the first meetings of your group.

Personal Issues in Starting a Group

I've talked to many men who were inspired by a book or by a friend's intimate sharing with them; they feel something in their heart, and then they want to start up or get into a men's group. But often they delay—they don't follow this feeling for a year or two.

The fear of intimacy with men can affect our lives in the most subtle ways! We may forget that a need for male connection was evoked, and simply go on with our busy lives. Or we may get discouraged because we don't know other men or how to contact them.

Three common tactics can help you continue working towards your goal of starting a men's group:

1. Create a schedule of goals. Make a list of the tasks which you must accomplish to make the group begin, using information in this chapter, and set action dates for each activity.

2. Create a support system for your efforts. Enlist family and friends to help you with your project. Often women are more sympathetic to men wanting to change and grow than other men, and they can help spread the word. Ask people to help you find other men and network. Ask them to remind of your goals and schedule. With a support system in place, you are already beginning to break out of isolation. You can talk to these allies about your fears and resistances, as well as your hopes.

3. Write down on a piece of paper two simple sentences which describe your reasons for wanting a men's group, such as "I want to become a powerful, creative, loving man. I want to learn more about relationship as a man." Keep it simple and focus on the benefits for you, not on processes or political-social theory. Tell the members of your support system these objectives. These friends will find it easier to help you if they know exactly what you want. The universe responds more precisely to our visions when we are clear about what we want.

Locating Men

My experience has shown me two general concepts about starting a group. People you know are more likely to enter into a group situation with you than people you don't know. And men are more easily attracted to your group if you can state your vision clearly. So make up your goal statements and begin talking to your friends and support system.

If you have to advertize, or extend your efforts to broader-based community groups, here are some methods which have worked in the past:

1. Utilize local networks of men: check the list of resources at the end of this book.

2. Attend men's events in your area; see if you can host a table and get men who are interested in a group to sign up on a list.

3. Put ads in your local alternative papers: your politically correct or artistic weekly. Check these papers for ads placed by other men.

4. Go to places where people are interested in transformation, recovery, or social consciousness, such as book stores, colleges, recovery houses, or cafes. Put out sign up sheets.

5. Go to local progressive churches, especially Unitarian. Many have monthly men's meetings.

6. Sponsor a local men's talk or speaker at a book store or coffee house.

7. Get creative; hire a biplane to pull a sign over the nearest beach or ice-skating rink.

Maintaining the Vision

When you create a group, you must remain true to your inner vision and communicate it clearly to other men. But there is a balancing act here, because other men will come to you with their own vision and hopes. Opportunity exists here for a co-creative act of listening, visioning, and collaborating. Tension can also arise if men don't know what their own goals and the group goals are, or if power struggles emerge over whose vision will be implemented.

In a group I was in several years ago, we brought in three new members within a few months. The group had been together for a long time, doing ritual and art activities together, and while I liked these processes, I felt a need for more direct communication and honesty. The new members did also. Tom, one of the new members, was telling a story about reconnecting with his father. He had written him a letter, then gone to see him after a painful separation of several years. We were asking him questions about his intentions for the new relationship, and about how the visit had gone, when Frank, one of the older members interrupted angrily and said, "Hey, we're all psychologizing this guy. I don't want to do this. This isn't therapy..."

Tom looked puzzled and said. "I thought they were just expressing their interest."

Frank's comments sparked an important group discussion, and he revealed that he really didn't want to have long personal conversations in our group, he wanted to do more art and poetry. The group members took a deep breath together, and realized that conflict was happening.

Several months later, Frank left the group, saying that he was ready for a change. We never heard more from him about the "psychologizing," or personal sharing, but I thought that our increased interest in this sparked his departure.

Frank's absence still leaves a hole in my heart, but I also enjoyed that group's deepening over the next months and years. And it showed me the painful but real lesson that members' needs are not all the same.

Here is a list of key questions for thought and discussion when the group is starting and interviewing possible members.

1. What kind of group do you want to create?

2. How long do you see yourself being in a group? Three months, six months, one year, three years, forever?

3. What experience have you had in other groups: men's, therapy, recovery, etc.? What about this previous experience do you want to have again, and what do you want to change or heal?

4. What kind of commitment are you willing to make: weekly, biweekly, monthly? Will you be on time? What times and days are best for you?

5. What method of leadership do you want for the group? Do you want a rotating leader or a permanent one? What are your issues about leadership, authority, and control? Are you willing to make your answers to these questions part of the group conversation?

6. What degree of involvement do you want with members outside of the group meetings? Do you want to make friends to socialize with, or just see members in the meetings?

The group's creator (or creators) must recognize that they will want to control the group. Groups pose a never-ending challenge; it's so hard to control them! Other members will have strong images and feelings about how the group will operate. You can count on their creativity and commitment. And on the fact that issues of power will emerge sooner or later. The group has to talk about these key issues openly, or the group will fragment with bad feelings.

There is bound to be some healthy friction between men as they meet and say what they want. As the group meets for the first few months, there will often be some turnover. The group has to define how the members want to interact with each other, and not everyone can be satisfied.

Members create their own exercises, their own shared history and trust. They go to workshops and bring back new ideas and hopes. The group will inevitably evolve over time.

CHAPTER 7

STAGES IN THE GROUP'S LIFE
THE BEGINNING

We will always find the first meetings of a group exciting, frightening, and challenging. We come together bringing all our fears from past men's events (fraternity hazings, army drinking parties, high school football teams) where we were hurt or maybe shamed for being vulnerable. All these painful episodes and memories reside somewhere in the room when we meet. As much as we want to let go of these memories, we will also want to control group process, so we don't have to be vulnerable until we build up some trust.

When I began leading groups, I wanted to be in control, so that the group would work "right" and so that the members would get the "proper" experience. What that meant, of course, was I was afraid to be vulnerable and say when I didn't know what to do next. I needed to appear "together," so I could stay safe. In this phase of my leadership I thought I had to manage the group carefully, so that members would feel good about the group. (And thus I could feel good about myself.)

Over time, I learned to trust group process and the members more. I began to let go, to let the group take care of itself, in terms of deciding on and doing activities, and even in intervening with, and making comments, to other members. But most important, I let go of holding myself back from the group, and of attempting to create a positive image of myself in their eyes. I started sharing my own life events more in the group, my thoughts, doubts, and feelings while I was with them.

Because of my belief in the importance of men's community, I realized I had to be in the group more, instead of playing the role of a therapist-observer. This is also an issue of timing. After the group has built up cohesion and trust between group members and between members and leaders, the time is ripe for more personal sharing by the facilitator.

And I know that whenever I join a group or a project, I am anxious, and this anxiety shows itself in different ways. I want to please the other members of the group, and sometimes I make jokes to diffuse my own fear. All of us, in the beginning stages of a group, will resort to old defensive patterns to keep people away, to control how vulnerable we will become.

One time several years ago, my men's group interviewed a new man. The whole evening he was there with us, he spent drawing a picture on a big pad in his lap. Finally one of the other members said, "Tim, what are you doing?" Tim said, "Oh, just trying to sketch out some ideas I had about..." Needless to say, we were not impressed with his willingness to be present, and we didn't invite him to stay.

I use this example because we all resist intimacy in some way. Many men will ask a thousand questions before they commit to a group, and most of the questions revolve around one or two central issues: Will I get hurt? Will the group love and accept me if I really show myself? If the group can talk about these issues in depth, great awareness and transformation can occur.

I begin in Chapter 7 with a group of exercises designed to help the group get started with clear intentions and a clear vision, with some simple group activities (mostly discussions), and with brief rituals to open and close the group. This section of exercises could take six to ten meetings to complete, since the discussion questions raised here could each take a two-hour meeting or more to complete. I recommend taking time on each one, until members feel in accord with the vision of the group and their intentions to explore psychological dynamics that will inevitably emerge in a group.

For easy reference, each exercise here and in other chapters is labeled as a discussion, a creative arts process, or a ritual.

GROUP CHECK-IN   DISCUSSION

DESCRIPTION

This basic activity provides a safe way for men to tell their ongoing stories to the group. Although it seems simple, the activity is so valuable that some groups do it to the exclusion of other exercises. A quality of listening and of support in it is deeply nourishing to us.

STEPS

1. The leader for the night starts the group in the usual way.

2. Optional: The leader can start with a short guided meditation in which he invites the men to breathe into their bodies, to let go of the errands of the day, and to find the deep truth that they want to share tonight.

3. Each man takes five to fifteen minutes (depending upon the agreement that night) to tell group members on how his life is going. He can talk about anything he wants for that period of time; the group and the leader should help the man emphasize the emotional content of his experience.

4. Optional: Sometimes after each man shares, the group can take a few minutes to give him feedback.

5. The next man takes his turn, until all men have checked-in.

6. The group leader then closes the group in the usual way.

COMMENTS

What seems like a simple exercise takes on an emotional richness over time, as men find listeners and supporters for their life's pains and victories. This acknowledgment nurtures a man's need for love and affection, and helps him feel better about himself and his life.

I look forward to my group's bi-monthly check-ins, since I draw strength from watching men I know so well wrestle with their life issues with courage and awareness. I know that I don't have to hide myself there; all my awkward, embarrassing, weak parts can be acknowledged, as well as my power and my successes.

Often a man's issue will create group discussion or evoke group support, or often a man will have strong feelings while he is sharing. These developments can effect how long a man's story will be. A solution to timing problems is to have a clear ground rule: Everyone will take ten minutes. And then the group should agree if someone wants more time. Otherwise some men will start feeling anxious about their turn, who's in charge, etc.

GROUP BEGINNINGS AND ENDINGS   RITUAL

DESCRIPTION

These short exercises open and close the group in a conscious way. Following these practices, or others you develop, helps men to remember that we have come together for a special time and special focus. This remembering feeds our soul's desire for intimacy.

STEPS

1. Group meetings may start or end with all men standing together and hugging each other. At the group's end, any man who has shared deeply or who wants support can enter the middle. Men gather around him and touch or hug him.

2. The group may begin or end with a period of silence; men either look at each other or close their eyes.

3. The group may begin or end with a sitting or standing circle of men holding hands for several minutes.

4. The group may begin or end with a chant (OOOMMMM; AAHHH-HH or a phrase created by the group.)

5. The leader can start with a short guided meditation in which he invites the men to breathe into their bodies, to let go of the errands of the day, and to find the deep truth that they want to share tonight.

6. The leader for the night ends by saying, "Well I guess that's it." Or "Go Niners, Go Giants, What about them Lakers, or See You." (This is a joke.)

7. Optional: The group leader can check the creative arts section for endings which use sound, movement, or play.

COMMENTS

Groups will experiment with various beginnings and endings until they find ones that members connect with. It is important to use a consensual process and to let group members check-in from time to time as to how the openings and closings are going.

Check-in and ritual beginnings mark a change; we create a boundary against world, with its quick pace and incessant errands. We slow down and enter our hearts and our bodies in a new way. We find out what our souls want to say to us.

USING THE TALKING STICK   RITUAL

DESCRIPTION
This exercise also creates a ritualized, focused atmosphere in which men can tell their story. The talking stick allows men to talk without interruption. Men long to be deeply heard and witnessed, in ways that their parents might not have been able to do for them.

STEPS
0. Prior to meeting, the group decides that it wants to use a talking stick, and makes one. One man or the group can create the stick. (See below)

1. The leader for the night starts the group in the usual way. He describes the purpose of the talking stick (as he holds it aloft) and the simple rules. Only the person with the talking stick shares; others pay attention. The leader decides if the men have unlimited time with the stick or five, ten, or fifteen minutes.

2. Then the leader puts the stick in the center of the circle. When a man feels ready to speak, he picks up the stick and begins.

3. When he is done, he puts the stick back in the center of the room and the group falls silent till the next man picks up the stick and shares whatever he wants with the group.

4. After everyone has shared, or time has elapsed, the leader closes the group in the usual way.

COMMENTS
Men's groups have been adapting this stick ritual from Native Americans for at least a decade. It changes the atmosphere within which men are speaking. The stick helps us to let go of our ever-present mind-chatter and focus our attention on the speaker. This deep attentiveness often touches the heart of the speaker.

The group can choose to imbue the stick with blessings, prayers, and intentions while they are creating it or beginning to use it. For example, the first time it is used in the circle, each man can say something like, "Let this stick always remind me to tell the truth...to take a risk, etc." This creative process (decorating the stick with different paints, artifacts, feathers, etc.) can take a whole group meeting. This artistic experience can bond the group. While the members make the stick, men can say what various adornments mean to them, and what their intentions are when they use the stick.

MATERIALS
Sticks, feathers, colored yarns, bones, paints, shells, etc.

CREATING THE GROUP   DISCUSSION

DESCRIPTION

These exercises help men to talk about group agreements and under-
standings. Agreement about these topics creates a set of benchmarks that
group members can refer back to as the group continues. The discussion
of such core topics creates group safety and cohesion.

STEPS

1. The leader for the night starts the group in the usual way.

2. He begins a group discussion by asking one of the following questions.

   A. What kind of group do I want to be in? (Refer to Chapter 6 for
   possible answers.)

   B. What is my commitment to the group: time, attention, etc.? Will
   I make group participation a priority?

   C. What kind of leadership do I want in the group? Am I willing to
   be a leader? Will I be willing to deal with my issues about leadership in an honest, non-blaming way?

3. Men go around the circle and answer whichever question the group
   leader has recommended.

4. Open dialogue can follow after the whole group has commented on
   a question.

5. The leader closes the group in the usual way.

COMMENTS

Please refer to Chapter 3 for more information about Questions B and C;
these last two topics come from the list of issues that cause the group to
have communication problems.

In Chapter 9, I bring up these same questions again, because the group is
always working with them, either consciously or unconsciously.

The discussions on this page should take two to three meetings, if each
question is asked and investigated deeply. The group should take its time.
Care taken here will help solve a lot of questions and problems that can
come up later in the group.

INTERPERSONAL DYNAMICS   DISCUSSION

DESCRIPTION
These exercises help men to talk about personal dynamics which will emerge as the group meets. The power of groups is that they magnify old communication and personality patterns, in an environemnt where we can observe them and change them. The open discussion of such core topics creates group safety and cohesion.

STEPS
1. The leader for the night starts the group in the usual way.

2. He starts a group discussion by asking one of the following questions.

   A. What is my greatest fear in this group? What might go wrong that would hurt me?

   B. What method would I use to stay isolated from the group? (Humor, sarcasm, criticism of others, spacing out, not coming.)

   C. What family patterns do I feel are evoked by my participation in the group?

   D. Who dominates the airtime in the group? What is he talking about during this time? How do the group members feel at these times? Interested, passive, angry, bored?

   E. Are men committed to truthtelling instead of blaming? Are they willing to practice being self-responsible?

3. Men go around the circle and answer whichever question the group leader has recommended.

4. Open dialogue can follow after the whole group has commented on a question.

5. The leader closes the group in the usual way.

COMMENTS
Please refer to Chapter 3 for more information about topics B-E. This particular exercise requires men to talk about the inner experience of the group, and it asks the members to be vulnerable and non-blaming.

In Chapter 9, I bring up these same questions again, because the group is always working with them, either consciously or unconsciously. These discussions should take several weeks, if each question is asked and investigated deeply. The group should take its time. Care taken here will help solve a lot of questions and problems that can come up later in the group.

CHAPTER 8

STAGES IN THE GROUP'S LIFE
GOING DEEPER

In the second stage of the group's journey, men feel excitement, deepening trust and new depths of friendship. Often group members are exhilarated that great obstacles such as fear and logistics were overcome and that they actually can meet together and bond.

I remember reading in Allen Ginsberg's journals about the long, cross-country journeys he, Jack Kerouac, Gary Snyder and others would take to meet. He wrote something like, "We would hitchhike across America to talk to a friend." In Ginsberg's comment I heard his great loneliness, and also the bond he shared with his fellow travelers and dharma bums, a bond in which their hearts had been touched by some capacity for truth or joy or creativity in their brothers. A heart once touched by a kindred spirit will never be the same. Many men like myself have experienced these powerful emotions of bonding and brotherhood through men's meetings.

In the early 1980's many of the men in the Bay Area who attended retreats together created a group called the Golden Gate Men's Council. We drove from all over the Bay Area to a small community center in San Francisco one Sunday a month, and well I remember the fondness and even hilarity with which we greeted each other after a month's absence.

We were new to such intense male friendships, and we created funny rituals and awkward activities, as we experimented with community building. One time at a Golden Gate Men's Council meeting, my friend Doug and I tried in one afternoon to bring back a ten-thousand-year-old tradition of initiation, a tradition that the men there agreed we had lost in our childhoods, somewhere between the "Ozzie and Harriet" show and Little League.

Doug and I dressed up in robes, and we wore the bones of cattle over our heads. We asked the thirty men at the meeting to line up blindfolded all around the walls of this small gym. We tried to terrorize them by blowing conch shells in their ears and jostling them, because we knew that indigenous tribal rituals contained the threat of death, or at least embarrassment, for the boys. But unfortunately most of the men there knew when they took off their blindfolds, they'd still be in the gym. No lives were at stake. Doug and I wondered why these guys weren't permanently transformed by our attempts to bring back ritual into their lives. Then we sat down together to a lunch of spaghetti, after which we played volleyball with terrific zeal and little skill.

In the second stage of the group's life, besides the excitement, men are testing each other. How safe is it? How much of myself can I reveal? As we share secrets about our lives, we look around the room, afraid to be so vulnerable. Will we be received, or will someone shame us, and recommit the abuses we've all experienced in the past? There is only one way to find out.

As my friend and colleague, Lou Dangles, suggested, the group is deepening into contact in at least three different ways. Personal stories and discussions bring the group together, and they prepare the ground for direct sharing and interactive work between men, the second form of depth. Ritual work provides a context for men to work and bond in; we see ourselves as part of the great forces and mysteries of the universe, not just guys stuck in our personal dramas and traumas, but men wrestling with important issues of community, creativity, and compassion. This larger picture brings yet a different form of depth.

In the exercises for Chapter 8, I have included a number of discussions, creative arts activities, and rituals. A couple of the discussion activities encourage direct dialogue between group members. These direct dialogues prepare the way for activities which help solve group problems in Chapter 9.

HONEST DIALOGUE   DISCUSSION

DESCRIPTION

Group members give each other honest feedback about their relationships. The practice of truthtelling has a powerful effect on men's ability to communicate within, and outside of, the group setting.

STEPS

1. The group leader starts the group in the usual way.

2. The leader asks for a volunteer to enter the circle.

3. Optional: The leader asks for a brief period of silence, during which everyone holds the intention that the feedback given and received will be for each man's benefit and growth.

4. The volunteer faces each of the others one by one and says, "Tell me something you like about me and something that you have trouble with."

5. Each man responds honestly, talking about his own experience of the man who has volunteered, and talking without judgement or blame.

6. The volunteer in the middle waits until all the men have talked to him and then responds to the feedback.

7. The group leader ends the group in the usual way.

COMMENTS

Because of the way most of us were raised, we need practice hearing other peoples' truth and accepting it. And we spend so much energy holding back truth from our friends and partners. This simple activity takes a lot of practice, and I have given more complex instructions in Chapter 9.

Depending upon the amount of time available, another man can volunteer to go into the middle, or the group can continue next time with another volunteer.

This activity was suggested by Bob Myer, San Anselmo, CA.

HEALING THE SHAME BOY WITHIN   DISCUSSION

DESCRIPTION

Men can tell old secrets, and feel the relief of exposing true parts of themselves to others. We waste so much energy keeping secrets about the times when we of feel weak or ashamed.

STEPS

1. The leader starts the group in the usual way.

2. The leader makes a brief introduction, describing the purpose of the evening as an inquiry into shame. Then he says, "Take a few moments and breathe into your body. Remember a time this week when you felt shame for your actions, or in the presence of someone else."

3. The leader asks the following questions slowly, pausing after each one, while the men are silent. "What were the bodily sensations which you felt? How did you learn to experience shame in this way? Do you remember feeling shame like this as a child? Where were you: how old, who was with you? Did you talk about it then? Now take a few deep breaths and return to the room."

4. One by one, men go around the circle and answer the questions.

5. After all have shared, the group can have a general discussion about what are the common themes, feelings, histories, etc.

6. Optional: Using the creative movement exercises, each man can imagine what his shame boy walks like, talks like, and looks like. Then each member can act out his shame boy, letting him speak to the rest of the group. The shame boys can talk to each other and interact.

7. Optional: The leader can end with a blessing ritual so that men know that even though they have these uncomfortable feelings, they can be loved and appreciated.

8. The leader ends the group in the usual way.

COMMENTS

Shame, a very deep feeling for men, is one that we keep a secret. Shame is elicited when we expose a part of ourselves that we do not want to show in public. It is healing to begin to let shame out into an accepting environment. We have heard so much, "Don't be a crybaby. Don't be a wimp, fag, girl, sissy." Our group shows us that we still merit love, even when we feel weak, vulnerable or incompetent, as we all do at times.

GENDER ROLES: HOW WE BENEFIT, HOW WE SACRIFICE

DISCUSSION

DESCRIPTION

The training we received to be men has a tremendous impact on our social, personal, and economic lives. It is important for us to take note of how we have benefited and how we have suffered from these powerful cultural messages and from the behaviors that have resulted from them.

STEPS

1. The leader for the night starts the group in the usual way.

2. Optional: The leader starts a general discussion about what the men see as the main differences between men and women in the group's social circles. What are the traits that the men seem good at, or weak at? What do women seem to do well, compared to men?

3. The leader then directs the conversation into a more personal vein. Each man answers the questions: What character traits or behaviors do I have as a man which have developed differently than those of the women I know? What have I lost in my life for not having had other characteristics supported?

4. After men answer these questions, the leader asks, "What is the personal benefit of having the masculine traits which each man has identified? (This list will be different for each man.) How do they help me in relationship, in work, in social life? How do they hurt me? What part of my life or my soul is not developed when I act from within my conditioning?

5. Optional: How have these traits affected the women in my life?

6. Optional: Men can role play their father's voices, or the cultural voices from different eras. For example, "What would your father say about men's and women's roles? Imitate his voice and posture and show us."

7. Each man takes an agreed amount of time, or the timing can be left open.

8. The leader closes the group in the usual way.

COMMENTS

These are large topics, worthy of being revisited several times. The leader should balance the importance of each topic with the need for men to share every night. He doesn't have to get through all the questions in one night. These discussions can reach into the depths of our self-concepts and beliefs. These questions provoke laughter, fear, anxiety, tears, guilt, and many other emotions.

For myself, much of my healing path has focused on freeing my deep essential qualities of joy, humor, courage, and dedication from the shackles of my adult male conditioning, which has limited my ability to express these qualities.

This discussion can be adapted to other important social or political issues. For example, if the group wants to work on the issue of racism, the questions could be rephrased: What character traits do I have as a --(pick one) European-American, Asian-American, African-American--that may have developed differently from other races? What is the personal benefit to me of having these traits? What is the cost to me? How have these traits affected men of other races?

MY NEXT CHALLENGE   DISCUSSION

DESCRIPTION
Men describe their next challenge or transition, especially the parts which
are difficult, painful, or confusing. They receive support, understanding
and group wisdom. Reaching out for support counteracts our superhero
fantasies. It puts us in touch with our vulnerability and our community.

STEPS
1. The leader starts the group in the usual way.

2. The leader for the night says slowly, "Close your eyes, breathe into
   your body. Feel yourself slowing down. Feel into the transitions
   which you are going through right now. It may be a transition with
   a relationship, a job, a vision, or a part of yourself. Let yourself feel
   the most important or most difficult challenge. What is the hardest
   part of this transition for you? What kind of support do you need to
   make it work the best for you? How is it like other transitions you
   have gone through in the past?"

3. One by one, each man shares what he has thought and felt, and the
   group gives him feedback about the process, about what they see
   for him in it, how they can help, etc.

4. Optional: The leader ends with a ritual in which each man makes a
   statement of intention and says it to the group, and the group gives
   him feedback about his enthusiasm, his forcefulness, his body language and the sound of his voice. The man can repeat the intention
   untill he convinces the group of his belief in himself.

5. The group leader closes the group in the usual way.

COMMENTS
We are so used to going through the most stressful times alone, in a form
of solitary confinement of the heart!

When the man states his intentions, it is powerful for him to stand in the
middle of the circle. The group can give feedback about body language
such as, "I hear you say the words, but your voice drops at the end and I
can't hear you." Or "The words seem to be coming from your head, not
your belly." The man can be asked to exaggerate his enthusiasm by ten
times when he is in the middle; this tactic raises energy!

This exercise lends itself to creative movement. Each of us has different
inner characters as we go through transition: adventurer, wimp, fearful
one, voice of our parents. Having the group play out these different characters is very powerful.

TRUTHTELLING IN PAIRS   DISCUSSION

DESCRIPTION

A truthtelling process allows men to deepen their connections with the other members by honest sharing with them. Each man is actively involved during the meeting.

STEPS

1. The group leader starts the group in the usual way.

2. Each man pairs up with a partner.

3. Optional: Each dyad can start with thirty seconds of silence so men can remember their intentions for truth and healing, or with thirty seconds of silent looking at their partner.

4. With the partner, each man answers these four questions in six to eight minutes. What do I like about you? How does this reflect on me? What don't I like about you? How does this reflect on me?

5. Then his partner answers the same four questions.

6. Then group members switch partners till everyone has spoken to everyone at the group for six to eight minutes. (Each dyad takes ten to fifteen minutes.)

7. Group members make a circle when all dyads have been completed and share insights and feelings. Men can also clear any feelings which may not have been fully expressed in the pairs, and can ask for help from the group in this process.

8. The group leader ends the group in the usual way.

COMMENTS

When we answer the question, how does this reflect on me? we understand better the conditioning which creates judgement in our mind. Our judgements of other men can usually be traced back to the hurt caused by an elder, a parent, or some other authority figure. Awareness of this conditioning is the first requirement for healing; intention to let go of judgement and connect is the second.

In this activity, group members practice a fundamental transformational tactic—taking the attention off what we judge in the other, and sending that intention or inquiry back into our own history. This practice makes us less reactive and more accepting.

This activity was suggested by John Bilney, Novato CA.

PHOTO OPPORTUNITY   DISCUSSION

DESCRIPTION
Through using photos of loved ones, men can touch deep feelings about their relationships, and we can practice expressing these truths. We need to work at regaining this skill.

STEPS
0. Prior to the meeting, men agree to bring pictures of loved ones who have died to the next meeting.

1. The leader for the night starts the group in the usual way.

2. One at a time, each man passes around the picture or pictures which he has brought. (Or puts the photographs on a table or altar near the group.)

3. The man shares the meaning of the picture, the feeling and memories in the relationship. How old was he in the picture? Who else is in the pictures with him? What do the configurations in the photos tell him about his family relationships?

4. When he feels complete, the next man shares, and so on around the group.

5. When the group has shared, the men can talk together about general themes, or feelings that have emerged.

6. Optional: Men can make an altar with the pictures and other sacred objects and bless and honor the relationships.

7. The group leader ends the group in the usual way.

COMMENTS
Strong feelings of love or loss can emerge during this activity. All of our relics carry such heartful memories, and as the men share in turn, a mood of connection and depth results.

A variation of this exercise involves men bringing in several childhood pictures of themselves. Many childhood patterns can be seen just in the collection of pictures: who is seen with whom, what are the various expressions of the family members, who is sitting next to whom, etc.

My wife and I were at my mother's house watching old home movies, and we saw a clip of my mother trying to kiss me when I was thirteen. I turned my head and moved my body from her in a way that Debra had seen many times in our relationship. I was embarrassed when I saw the movie, but also felt some forgiveness for how that pattern might have been started.

The exercise also works if everyone in the group brings a picture of the same family member: father, grandfather, brothers; then the conversation focuses on that specific kind of relationship.

This activity was suggested by Michael Ford.

MATERIALS
Photos of the agreed-upon family member.

HONORING THE KING   DISCUSSION

DESCRIPTION
This exercise gives men a chance to describe good qualities about themselves and others. Men often long for acknowledgment from their peers, but we don't have much regular practice in supportive communication with men.

STEPS
1. The leader for the night starts the group in the usual way.

2. Option: The leader or other men tell stories about kings, in history or mythology, so models of kingly behavior are shared. Or men can visualize kingly behavior they have seen recently.

3. Each man says briefly how he believes he has some kingly values and how he has demonstrated them in his life recently, either with group members or with others. Kingly values would be: discipline, kindness, sympathy, orderliness, generosity, etc. (Whatever you think they are.)

4. Other men in the group give him feedback as to whether or not they actually feel these virtues in him. What kingly attributes has he forgotten to ascribe to himself?

5. Optional: Men can continue this discussion to talk about the pain of not being honored, or acknowledged by their elders or mentors. What kind of goodness or success did they have as children which was not recognized in the way that they wanted?

6. Optional: This discussion could end with a blessing ritual so that the men could be deeply acknowledged by the other men in these good qualities.

7. The leader ends the group in the usual way.

COMMENTS
This can be a very evocative exercise, because our souls hunger for positive affirmation from men. But we are so used to subtle competition and subtle digs. Men can read chapters of Robert Moore and Douglas Gillette's book, *King, Warrior, Lover, Magician*, or listen to tapes by these men to prepare for this discussion. Men can use the same discussion format to talk over the other archetypal images mentioned in the book, such as the father, or the fool, or others.

This activity was suggested by Ronald Wallace, Glen Ellen, CA.

A MAN'S STORY   DISCUSSION

DESCRIPTION
Men tell each other their life story in one to two hours. Deepening our
friendships in this way builds trust and community.

STEPS
0. Prior to the meeting, the group decides that it wants to do this activity, and who will be the first storyteller. The storyteller assembles artifacts from his life: pictures, clothing, tapes, music, stories.

1. The leader starts the group in the usual way.

2. The storyteller for the night takes as long as he wants to present his life story to the group.

3. Optional: Men give responses about what they learned about him, and how they now have a better understanding of his behavior or emotional life.

4. Optional: The man may want to bless or forgive members of his family or people he has been affected by as he finishes his story. He may want to make some intentions about his future vision for his life.

5. The leader closes the evening with a blessing ritual for the man.

COMMENTS
When I have seen men tell their whole story uninterrupted, I have
watched them receive deeply the attention from their brothers in the
group. Everyone almost drinks in the new information, because it invariably brings with it new compassion and understanding for the man's
courage and his failures. After this activity, I have heard many men say,
often through their tears, "I never told it all the way through to anyone
before. No one ever heard the whole history like this."

Often groups will focus these long stories around themes: relationship,
work, fathers, mothers, wounds, victories, etc.

This activity was suggested by William Miller, Tiburon, CA.

MATERIALS
Pictures, clothing, tapes, music, stories which help tell the man's story.

JUST FOOLING AROUND   CREATIVE ARTS

DESCRIPTION
Men contact and heal that embarrassed foolish part of themselves which we have so often been told not to let out in public. We spend so much energy repressing our natural foolishness.

STEPS
1. The leader starts the group in the usual way.

2. All members in the group stand and spend a few moments getting in touch with the "Fool" part of themselves. The leader says, "Let yourself feel foolish. Now imagine letting your body express that inner foolish part."

3. When they feel moved, the members begin to act out the fool in their own ways: making funny noises, waving their arms and flying, spinning, tumbling, etc.

4. Optional: the group forms a circle and then lets each man act out his fool as the other men watch and appreciate him.

5. Then the group sits down together and the leader asks them to answer these questions in five minutes or so: What was the most foolish or stupid thing that you did in the last week? In your whole life?

6. After each man in the group tells a story, the group can share together insights or general statements about foolishness: What characteristics (in the setting or in the emotional life) are common when the fool inside comes out? Is being foolish associated with rebelliousness, embarrassment, or shame?

COMMENTS
This is a fun, active exercise. There is a great tradition of fool stories which most cultures share. Men can read up on these stories and share them as part of the evening.

Other internal characters can be invoked: the lover, the warrior, the king, the wounded child, the elder, the mother, the father, etc. And other types of questions can be asked: when have you really loved, or felt loved, in your life?

This activity was suggested by Scott King, Petaluma, CA.

MOVING, TOUCHING, GETTING CLOSE CREATIVE ARTS

DESCRIPTION

Men learn about personal boundaries through this exercise. We practice getting closer and farther away from other men and explore our comfort zone: how physically close can other men get to us?

STEPS:

1. The leader starts the group in the usual way.

2. Men stand and start moving around the room in silence in any way they want: walking, rolling, crawling, etc.

3. The leader says, "Notice what it is like to get closer to other men, and then further away. How does this feel in your body? Slow down and breathe. How does your body feel when you come right up against another man? How does it feel to move away?"

4. Optional: The leader can direct the men to slow down and close their eyes and move together, so that the group is in physical contact with each other. What does this feel like? Then members can experiment with moving back away from the group, with eyes open or shut. Where does each member feel safest—in the center of the group or on the edges? What does this feeling tell you about your family of origin? Were you safe in the middle, or on the edges of the family circle?

5. Then the group can reconvene in a circle and talk over feelings which have emerged.

6. The leader closes the group in the usual way.

COMMENTS

We hold men away from ourselves physically, and only feel safe when they come within certain distances of us. This activity helps us to see how we have learned to set these boundaries, and helps us to choose consciously when to let men into our lives.

Men need to be comfortable and safe while they are doing this exercise; loose clothing and carpeted rooms are ideal. Sometimes we have men say out loud their intentions for safety, such as "I agree that I can do this activity in total safety for myself and other men here."

The activity was suggested by Will Stapp, Petaluma, CA.

FOLLOW THE LEADER   CREATIVE ARTS

DESCRIPTION
This activity helps men to explore their feelings about leadership, power, and control in a safe and funny way. We men are constantly in friction with each other about who has the power, and who gets to do what they want. Awareness of these unconscious patterns helps heal this "power shortage."

STEPS:
1. The leader starts the group in the usual way.

2. Men stand and start moving around the room in silence in any way they want: walking, rolling, crawling, etc.

3. The leader says, "Notice what it is like to get closer to other men, and then further away. How does that feel in your body?"

4. After a while, the leader says, "Find a partner. Pick an A person and a B person. A person leads, B tries to follow. A person can move in any way that they want. B person tries to duplicate their every move."

5. After a few minutes, the leader says, "Notice what it is like to lead and to follow. Do either of you feel frustrated? Are you and your partner doing it right, or wrong? Do you subtly resist being the follower or the leader? What is it like to control or be controlled?"

6. The leader says, "Now switch roles. B leads and A follows."

7. After a while, the leader asks the same questions. He can also ask, "Which of these two experiences, of leading or following is the most familiar to you? What patterns at home or at work do you see in the exercise here? What patterns from your parents do you see now?"

8. After these different options are tried for ten to twenty minutes, the group can reform as a circle and talk over feelings which have emerged.

9. The leader closes the group in the usual way.

COMMENTS
Men need to be comfortable and safe while they are doing this exercise; loose clothing and carpeted rooms are ideal. Sometimes we have men say aloud their intentions for safety, such as "I agree that I can do this activity in total safety for myself and other men here."

This activity was suggested by Dr. Kathlyn Hendricks, Colorado Springs, CO.

EXPRESSIVE MOVEMENT — CREATIVE ARTS

DESCRIPTION

This exercise allows men to move together in new ways and to practice letting our whole bodies communicate. We carry so much emotional energy in our postures and our ways of moving which may not come out if we are just communicating verbally.

STEPS

1. The leader starts the group in the usual way.
2. The group members stand in a circle facing each other.
3. One at a time, a man moves his body and makes a noise which expresses how he is feeling in that moment.
4. The whole group makes the sound and movement, reflecting it back to the first man.
5. Then a second man moves his body and makes a sound, the group reflects it back to him, and so on around the group.
6. Optional: Men can mirror each other in pairs, instead of the whole group mirroring one man at a time.
7. The group can reform and talk over what they have expressed or felt.
8. The leader closes the group in the usual way.

COMMENTS

This activity can be used to start a group session. It allows members to check-in quickly and energetically. If you extend the movement and the feedback time, the activity can take the whole evening, especially if men start to interact and play with each other's movements.

Each member should pay attention when the others move. Watch for stiffness in parts of the body, the quality of the sounds made, movements that are half-made. We communicate on many levels when we make these movement check-ins, and the man taking his turn may benefit from questions about these topics.

This activity was suggested by Dick Moore, San Francisco, CA.

THIS IS MY JOB   CREATIVE ARTS

DESCRIPTION
This exercise helps men to communicate nonverbally, in this case about
what their job is and how they feel about it. Nonverbal expressions allow
for different truths and feelings to emerge.

STEPS
1. The leader starts the group in the usual way.

2. The group stands in a circle facing each other.

3. One at a time, a man expresses what his job is and how he feels
   about it by moving his body in the rhythm of work, and by making
   sounds or words.

4. The whole group makes the sound and movement, reflecting it back
   to the first man.

5. Optional: Men can bring other group members into the movement
   to enact the job or the stress that they feel doing it.

6. The rest of the members of the group follow in turn making sounds
   and movements which express the energy and the feeling of their
   work.

7. The group can reconvene and talk over what they have expressed.

8. The leader closes the group in the usual way.

COMMENTS
One time when we did this, a man moved his arms over his head and
pushed up, as if he were experiencing great pressure. He then pushed out
in two directions, and asked two men to push against him on either side.
He started yelling and pressing hard, saying "I can't do it all. I can't do
everything."

He then revealed how pressure at home and pressure at work were mount-
ing, and how he had been holding it within his body until this exercise.
The group asked him how he could release the pressure with the people
involved, and he committed to start, by talking to his wife and teenage
son and requesting their support and consideration.

This activity can be adapted to other topics: my relationship, my financial
position, my vision of the future, etc.

This activity was suggested by Peter Edwards, Forest Knolls, CA.

DRAMATIZING INNER CHARACTERS CREATIVE ARTS

DESCRIPTION
This exercise helps men to see the different characters which we have inside us. Changes in behavior can result from this understanding.

STEPS
1. The leader for the night starts the group in the usual way.

2. On a piece of paper, men write down thirty or forty adjectives which they think describe themselves. They then cluster eight or ten adjectives which seem to be related.

3. When they review these clusters, they close their eyes and find an image and a name for these four or five different characters: demented king, critical father, simpleton, stupid lover, twisted addict, etc.

4. The leader creates a brief visualization, in which he encourages each of the men to remember a time recently when one of these characters was "out" in the world and dominating their relationship with another person.

5. Each man recounts his story briefly and describes his character and how he talked, moved, and sounded.

6. The leader asks each man to dramatize this character. The men pair up in these characters and present little dialogues to the group, as if the two inner characters were trying to have a relationship, a friendship, or a business deal. The men continue presenting in pairs until they are laughing so hard they die laughing, or until fist-fights break out!

7. Optional: The leader ends the group by sending all the little inner people back home with the blessings of the group members.

8. The leader closes the group in the usual way.

COMMENTS
This exercise can be very evocative, because it exposes parts of ourselves which we often keep hidden. Men can present personal conflicts or relationship issues and take them apart in this way. Each of us has competing voices or attitudes, which we can characterize with images and characters, and which speak unconsciously when we are under stress.

This activity was suggested by Dr. Andrew Michaels, Berkeley, CA.

GROUP CONNECTIONS IN MOVEMENT   CREATIVE ARTS

DESCRIPTION
Men express their connections to other men in movement. Often nonverbal communication and movement allow men to get in touch with and clarify, feelings that they may not be fully conscious of.

STEPS
1. The leader for the night starts the group in the usual way.

2. The men form a standing circle. (Group drumming or background rhythms can be used.)

3. A man moves out into the middle of the circle, and draws another man into the circle with him.

4. In movement for a couple of minutes the men express nonverbally (moving their hands, feet, or bodies) how they feel about their relationship with the other man. They can move closer or further away as part of the expression.

5. After a few minutes, one of the men returns to the outer circle, and another man goes in. These two men express the energy and feelings of their relationship.

6. One by one, the group members go through this process until every man dances with every other man.

7. After the movement process is over, men sit down and describe verbally what they have learned, either moving with men or watching the interactions.

8. Optional: Since conflict and processing cannot always be finished in one night, the leader can end with a ritual blessing the men in these relationships. People can connect through ritual sometimes, even when they cannot connect personally.

9. The group leader closes the group in the usual way.

COMMENTS
When men start feeling and sharing the truth of relationship, it is important for the group leader and other men to help them tell the truth in a non-blaming way. This takes years of practice.

Men should carefully observe each other's movements during this activity. Are they making gestures (clenched jaw or fists, stamping feet) which they are not aware of? What is the tone of the movement: restrained, open, cut-off? Commenting on these observations helps us learn to read body language, an important relationship task.

BLESSING THE FATHER;   CREATIVE ARTS
RECEIVING BLESSINGS FROM THE FATHER

DESCRIPTION
This exercise allows men to feel gratitude for gifts from their fathers or elders; it helps us to be more gracious and to bless others more easily.

STEPS
1. The leader for the night starts the group in the usual way.

2. He starts a simple visualization activity. "Close your eyes, sit up straight, or lie down. Breathe slowly into the body. Let yourself think about the way you have received blessings from your father, or another important male elder."

   "Focus on one specific event. How did you feel at that time? What was the sound of your voice? Remember the sights and sounds and smells of the interaction. Did you feel centered and grounded, excited, scared, friendly? Were you aware of how you were feeling? What exactly were you receiving? Take some time to do that now."

3. "Could you fully receive the gift into your body and psyche? Take some time now to bring your father, or elder, into your heart, and thank him for his caring. Let yourself feel what he was feeling as he reached out to you, to care for you. See yourself as he must have seen you, and feel his generosity and love."

4. "Now if you can, bring an image of your father or your mentor, when he was kind to you, into your heart and say to him, 'Thank you. Thank you for loving me, for caring about me.' Let yourself feel your own gratitude and your affection for him. Offer some prayer or intention for his wellbeing, whether he is dead or alive. Bless his life and his intentions and his dreams, as he blessed yours."

5. "Now let go of the man in your heart, say goodbye to him in some way and let him go. Feel what it is like to let him go, to say goodbye, but let him go away now."

6. "Now bring yourself back into the room. Feel your feet on the floor. Take a few more breaths and rejoin the room."

7. Each man takes several minutes to share feelings and memories.

8. The leader ends the group in the usual way.

COMMENTS
Men often follow up this activity with a call or visit to their father or elder and report back to the group what they shared with that person. The activity can be used with mothers, brothers, sisters, and other family members.

Grieving Ritual   Ritual

Description
This ceremony allows each man to touch the grief he feels for family members or friends whom he has lost. Touching our grief connects us with the suffering of others and opens our hearts to feelings of empathy and compassion.

Steps
1. The group leader starts the group in the usual way.

2. The leader explains briefly how the ritual will be done and sets a tone of attentiveness. He makes an altar, including a bowl or receptacle for a small fire, and lights a candle. Room lighting should be dim. The leader can read some poems on death and loss. (See poetry texts in Chapter 11.)

3. He asks for several minutes of silence, during which men consider those they have lost and would want to pray for and honor. Group members write these names down on pieces of paper.

4. After several minutes, each man in turn simply says the name of the person out loud and burns the paper in the flame.

5. Optional: Each man could tell a short story about a particular time the deceased person was kind to him or connected with him, as the paper is burning.

6. When all the men have finished, the group returns to silence for several minutes.

7. Optional: Then the group can begin drumming softly and chanting sounds. They can begin saying or singing out the names of those they know who have died, including those mentioned today, other friends, ancestors, etc.

Comments
Men have been told over and over, "Big boys don't cry." Being with men who grieve deeply opens us up to the possibility of love and intimacy in our lives. This exercise should move along slowly, giving care and time to the feelings of love and loss which our culture often wants to ignore.

This activity was suggested by Lance Lowen.

Materials
Candle, pencil, piece of paper for each man, altar materials, something to burn paper in, or drums, photos or other remembrances.

BLESSING RITUAL RITUAL

DESCRIPTION

Men practice blessing each other and praying for each other. This ancient communal activity touches a place of hope and shared beliefs in men, and gives us courage in our own struggles.

STEPS

1. The leader for the night starts the group in the usual way.

2. Men take a few minutes to think of what they would like to bless in their lives, what they are thankful for.

3. There are several simple blessings which men can use. Men can stand quietly together, and one by one each man can mention someone or something which he wants to bless. Then the group can visualize that object or person in the middle of the circle, with each man offering silent or verbal prayers, or chanting "Ommm." Each man can offer prayers for other men's topics.

4. After the group has finished one round of blessings, men can go around again if there is time.

5. The leader for the evening can close the group after all rounds of blessing are completed.

COMMENTS

In this suffering world, there are no end of topics and people to pray for, or to ask blessings for: our health (especially in crisis), our family members, warring or starving people, and our leaders, etc.

WINTER SOLSTICE RITUAL   RITUAL

DESCRIPTION

This type of ceremony helps men to stay connected to the cycles of the sun and the earth, and of our own lives. In the darkness of winter, some things die and are seen no more, and other things are germinating, waiting to be born.

STEPS

1. The leader starts the group in the usual way. He places a lighted candle in front of each man, and the lights in the room are dimmed.

2. The leader (or other group members) bring in poetry or short readings on the theme of the winter solstice: grief, loss, transition, hope, expectancy. These are read to the group.

3. Then the group leader turns out the lights.

4. Going around the circle in turn, each man reflects on a loss, disappointment, or transition during the previous year. When he is done, he blows out his candle.

5. When the last man speaks and blows out his candle, the group sits in the darkness together for several minutes.

6. Then on another round, each man speaks of his intentions and hopes for the new year. After he speaks, he lights a candle.

7. Optional: After each man has spoken twice, the group can create a group poem or chant that condenses the many hopes and losses into a few images or phrases that the group can say together.

8. The group leader closes the group in the usual way.

COMMENTS

Staying in touch with the cycles of the sun has been important to men and women throughout history. The descriptions of the history of these solstice and equinox holidays makes fascinating, and sometimes chilling reading. Read *The Golden Bough* by Sir James Frazer; he describes the great lengths which cultures have gone to, to ensure the return of the sun gods and their heat and light.

At the equinoxes, the days and nights are equal in length, so balancing light against darkness, or any other two polarities (masculine-feminine, listening-speaking, etc.) are good topics.

This activity was suggested by Robin Lewis, Albany, CA.

LIFE TRANSITION RITUAL RITUAL

DESCRIPTION

This exercise allows men to participate in life transitions which we often do not communicate with others. It helps to create support for men who are going through stressful times.

STEPS

1. The group leader starts the group in the usual way.

2. The man who is going through the transition takes several minutes to tell the group what is happening in his life. He describes emotional, financial, environmental, family, and social factors. He then describes what he might need.

3. The man then goes around the circle speaking to each man, telling him about the feelings he has for him.

4. Members may respond to the man in transition, offering any support or insight they have before he moves on to the next person.

5. Optional: After the man goes around the room, giving his expressions and getting feedback and support, then the group checks in about what it felt like to go through the process together.

6. Optional: If the group wants to keep the focus on the man in transition, it can put him in the center of the circle and do one of several different activities: stand quietly together, with each man offering silent or verbal prayers for the man's health and success; chant "Ommm" together and hold positive intentions for the man's passage; pray and bless the man and his family as he goes through this transition.

7. Optional: The man can ask for specific forms of help from the group.

8. The group leader ends the group in the usual way.

COMMENTS

Often if a group member wants to take a significant amount of group time, he will call other members in advance, or announce his needs at the previous meeting.

This activity was suggested by Jay Starbuck, Petaluma, CA.

MINDFULNESS MEDITATION   RITUAL

DESCRIPTION

This exercise helps men to notice the contents of their own mind, and the ways we tend to identify ourselves as those contents, instead of as great souls with busy, busy minds. This dis-identification is a profound relief!

STEPS

1. The leader for the night starts the group in the usual way.

2. He says to the group, "Sit up as straight as you can, in a position which you can hold for ten minutes with little movement. Bring the attention to the sensations of the breath, to the rising and falling of the chest and belly, to the movement of air in the throat or past the nostrils. Try to keep your attention focused there. When thoughts come up, notice what they are, and bring the attention back to the breath. Notice what thoughts keep coming up, and then return to the breath."

3. After ten minutes, the leader ends the meditation, and men can share what they experienced when they sat with their thoughts, and as they returned to attention to their breath.

4. After five or ten minutes of talking, repeat steps two and three a few more times during the night.

5. Optional: The leader can end with a blessing ritual which acknowledges the presence of all these thoughts in all these minds, and for the healing which we all need.

6. The leader ends with the usual closing.

COMMENTS

For best results, men should do this activity every day for the rest of their lives, like good Buddhists.(Joke) There are many variations on this basic mindfulness meditation: see books by Jack Kornfield.

The first time I meditated, I realized that all these convoluted thoughts I produce constantly are different from who I really am: a great soul who thinks thoughts on a regular basis, so I can practice detaching from them and becoming myself: a man who is generous, powerful, wise and loving. Since I began meditating fourteen years ago, I have learned a little better to express these qualities.

MATERIALS

A mind.

INVESTIGATING RACISM   DISCUSSION

DESCRIPTION
Racism tears apart the fabric of our culture. It shows itself in thought patterns, as well as in overt actions. In this exercise, men can acknowledge their racist judgements and thoughts, and this acknowledgement helps to heal the deep divisions between the races.

STEPS
1. The group leader starts the group in the usual way.

2. He begins a simple visualization. "Sit up straight or lie down comfortably. Imagine that a black man—Asian man—Hispanic man—European man (pick one) joins the group. You see him enter the room for his first meeting. Let yourself see him come towards the group, towards you. What does your body feel as you see him moving towards you?"

3. "What feelings come up in you about this man, just because of his racial background? What thoughts and feelings come up about yourself? What thoughts do you have about your group if he joins? How do you think the group might change if this man joins?"

4. "Let yourself think about the previous relationships (friends, schoolmates, neighbors, or work colleagues) you have had with members of this race? What has been the emotional quality of these relationships? Remember one significant interchange with someone of the new member's race? How did this experience affect your relationships, and your expectations about relationship with the new man in the group?"

5. "What judgements or racial thoughts have you carried in you as a result of your family or cultural history? What are the unmentionable thoughts that you carry inside about members of this race?"

6. After the visualization, the group members can check-in about any of these images or thoughts.

7. After a discussion, members can create a simple healing ceremony, which acknowledges these racial judgements and thoughts. Then the members can set intentions to work on them in specific ways.

COMMENTS
This exercise assumes that your group is predominantly of one race. If members of different ethnic backgrounds are already present, you can decide together how to do the visualization, and you can have direct dialogues, using some of the activities in Chapter 9, to educate yourselves about your thoughts about other racial groups and your intentions.

CHAPTER 9

STAGES IN A GROUP'S LIFE
PLATEAUS AND PROBLEMS

As months go by, the group can begin to feel stale and dull. Sometimes a new member brings in excitement, or doing new activities can help, but eventually, my experience has shown me, the group has to move towards introspection.

Members have to do a "gut-check" and ask themselves if they like what the group is doing. This self-analysis scares members. It forces them to look deeply at their communication habits and their ways of being intimate and being distant. It also requires direct conversation between members.

This cycle of group life can lead to great awareness and revived interest in the group, and to learning new skills that are invaluable outside the group. If however, group trust and safety have not been created, and if men don't feel bonded, the group can fragment. This is a tough balancing act, but it is one that we do all the time with other relationships too, so we have some experience with this judgement call.

A couple of years ago, a friend, Andrew, was starting up a group with some of his buddies. After a few meetings, I called and asked him how it was going, and he said, "I can't believe how angry I have gotten...First of all this guy, I hardly know him. Didn't come two times ago. He called in to say that his girlfriend wanted some quality time and it had to be on that night. We had just agreed on meeting nights the week before...But that wasn't all. There's this other guy in the group, very successful doctor...he talks all night. Whenever there is a pause in the action, he jumps in. He takes up all the time. I don't get to talk..."

I asked him if he felt like he could tell these guys about the problems he was having. He said, "No. It just makes me want to stay home." I knew that he had joined the group to get support about issues with his teenage kids, and to practice interacting with people, so I said, "Do you see how the group is doing its work? You feel like people can't hear you. You feel abandoned by this man. And you don't know how to talk to them without blowing up, just like your father used to do with you...I'd say that the group is giving you a perfect opportunity to work on the issues that you said you're there for."

"Yeah, I guess so," Andrew said. "It's just hard to be vulnerable with this group of guys. I've known some of them for a long time, I don't know how to bear my heart to them. There is such fear in me. And of course, I don't want to talk about that, I'd rather be mad at the others. That is my pattern of protection."

Andrew's group had originally met to talk about specific topics, but inevitably group dynamic issues were raised. And Andrew was wrestling with fundamental problems of safety and trust, within this group of powerful men. My experience shows me that unless Andrew's group could communicate some of these deeper group experiences, the members would reach a plateau. Eventually general topics will not hold the group together, because of the unspoken conflicts which need to be aired.

Several clear signals indicate when a group is on a plateau.

1. Men are complaining outside the group about certain members, or about the way the group is working.

2. Men leave the group meetings feeling uninvolved, or there are long periods at the meetings when men are bored.

3. Men begin missing group sessions; other life commitments become more important.

4. There is more expression of anger at the meetings, sometimes with inexplicable causes.

5. There are no activities or conversations that bring men into direct contact with each other, so a backlog of uncommunicated feelings builds up. It is important to remember that what may be a plateau for one man, a time when the group feels slow and stagnant, may be a period of quiet calm and nurturing for other members. These divergent voices must all be heard, so that men can reflect on and communicate how the group is working for them.

The exercises in this chapter build on some of the interactive exercises in Chapter 8. They ask men to tell the truth to each other and about the group itself.

For example, in one group, we spent three sessions in a row going around the room and saying to each other, "Blank, something I have been meaning to say to you for a long time but I haven't been able to is....." Many deep hurts surfaced, and some men expressed their pain and anger. But the group provided a place for an exciting experiment in conflict resolution, and after the emotional clearing, we felt much more bonded and open to truthtelling.

Men should hold in their hearts the vision that they can clear their judgements and old unspoken communications in a group setting and thereby become closer to the other men.

After ten years of group work, I know that groups will deepen as they begin to deal with conflict directly. The exercises in this chapter give tools for this important exploration. They help members confront their own deeply unconscious patterns of withholding love and truth from others. Sometimes meetings which use these exercises can be painful, but if men enter into them with a heart full of hope and forgiveness, and with a mood of exploration, they can create deeper bonds.

Here are some tips for these interactive processes.

1. These exercises should have a designated facilitator for the night, since each man can get caught up in his own emotional reactivity. An outside observer is very helpful.

2. When doing one of these exercises, the leader should help participants take the focus off the other man whom the member is talking to and about. The member should concentrate on his own bodily-emotional experience. One of my teachers, Dr. Gay Hendricks, says the goal is to make statements from our own truth which are inarguable, such as the difference between "You let me down," and "When you act that way, I feel sad and distant, and my chest hurts." The second statement is strictly my own truth—to the bone.

3. Members should always ask themselves what past wound or hurt in their personal history is being activated, if they

are feeling reactive to another man, if they want to judge or blame him, or if they are angry with him? These face-to-face talks go much better when each person is trying to plumb the depths of his own patterns of emotional experience.

4. The facilitator for the night must pay attention to the types of statements that are being made: are they inarguable personal truths, or are they accusatory or blaming? The easiest way to tell is to listen to the response of the other man.

GROUP CLEARING   DISCUSSION

DESCRIPTION
Group members clear any communications withheld from each other, within a format that contributes to safety and personal growth. This exercise helps men practice the skills of truthtelling and conflict resolution.

STEPS
1. The group leader starts the group in the usual way.

2. Through a visualization, group members are asked to determine if there are any unexpressed, withheld communications with any other members. For example, the group leader can say, "Close your eyes, take a few deep breaths. Picture each man in the group, and feel your connection with him. Do you feel open to him? If you feel closed to someone, ask yourself, 'Is this okay with me? Is there anything which I need to say to feel closer or more connected to this man?'"

3. The group leader explains the format for sharing. (Steps 4-9)

4. One member who is withholding says the name of the man he needs to talk to. These two men face each other.

5. The first man asks permission to tell his truth.

6. If the responder says yes, then the man states his communication, his feelings, and the effect of the withhold on their relationship.

7. The man listening asks for clarification and says, "Is there anything else you need to tell me?" If so, the first man tells it.

8. When the first man feels complete, he says so.

9. Then the second man responds, in a non-blaming, responsible way.

10. When the men feel complete, another pair can enter the circle and follow the same procedure.

11. The group leader ends the group in the usual way.

COMMENTS
This exercise should be done with the intention of cleaning up communication blocks and creating more intimacy. The consent and intention of the parties are critical. The leader's role is to provide safety and help the men stay within the guidelines that they have agreed upon. This model can also work for someone who has trouble with the group itself: its format, style, communications, etc.

If the men cannot agree to clear their feelings, they can talk about their fear, or suggest another time when they can talk.

This exercise was suggested by Eric Grabow, Berkeley, CA.

TELLING THE HONEST TRUTH   DISCUSSION

DESCRIPTION
This exercise gives men another safe structure for speaking deep truth to members of the group.

STEPS
1. The group leader starts the group in the usual way.

2. One man volunteers. One at a time each man tells the volunteer what he likes about him.

3. After the group finishes, the man responds about how it felt to hear positive descriptions about himself.

4. Then the group makes another round, giving the man honest feedback about personality traits or behaviors that he might want to work on, ways he defends against intimacy, and advice or support for particular issues.

5. After the group has finished with this round of feedback, the man responds.

6. Then the group talks briefly about the members' own experiences talking and listening in this way.

7. Optional: The leader can have another man go through the process that same night or wait for the next meeting.

COMMENTS
This potentially powerful exercise needs a leader who will encourage honesty that is not attacking, but not falsely nice either. It is valuable to observe the man receiving feedback. Is he breathing in a shallow way? (This can indicate a defense against deep feeling.) Groups members can encourage him to breathe deeper and to tell the truth.

This exercise was suggested by Ron Chicione, Palo Alto, CA.

CREATING AND AVOIDING INTIMACY IN THE GROUP

DISCUSSION

DESCRIPTION

This exercise shows men clearly how they reach out to other men, and how they resist them. We need practice in understanding these two habits.

STEPS

1. The leader for the night starts the group in the usual way.

2. He starts a simple visualization activity. "Close your eyes, sit up straight, or lie down. Breathe slowly into the body. Let yourself think about the way you have interacted with the men tonight, in greeting them, in joining with them in the circle, in carpooling, etc. Feel yourself reaching out to them, or holding back from them. How did you reach out to men, and how did you hold yourself back?

   Concentrate on one interaction with a man. How did you feel? What did your voice sound like to you? Were you leaning towards, or holding yourself away from him? Did you make eye contact? What unconscious habits of connecting were you using?"

3. "Now go back a little further in time. How are these habits familiar to you from other times during which you are trying to connect with people? How did you learn to connect this way? Do you remember any incidents from childhood in which you acted this way? What part of your personality do you share? What part do you hold back?"

4. "Now bring yourself back into the room. Feel your feet on the floor. Take a few more breaths and rejoin the room."

5. Each man takes several minutes to share the patterns which he saw in himself. He can invite others to give him feedback about his connection with them.

6. Optional: In Chapter 8, there are exercises on playing out parts of the personality. Many inner characters show up when we meet other men: the pleaser, the ingratiator, the one who wants to impress, etc. Some creative drama with these inner characters can be revealing.

7. The group leader closes the group in the usual way.

COMMENTS

This is a great exercise for either starting the group (in the first few meetings) or later, after the group has been meeting for a while. The patterns of intimacy and defendedness that show up here will be the same patterns that each man uses in other relationships. Awareness helps them to change.

GROUP RULES, GROUP TABOOS   DISCUSSION

DESCRIPTION

This exercise helps men to understand the communicaton practices which have developed in the group. They can then decide if they want to continue them, or change them.

STEPS

1. The leader for the night starts the group in the usual way.

2. He uses the simple visualization process. "Close your eyes, sit up straight, or lie down. Breathe slowly into the body. Let yourself think and feel, what are the rules that we follow in this group? What are the conscious and unconscious rules which dictate the ways that we will act? Which of these rules do you like, or would you never break?

3. "What are the rules that you break subtly, or that you hate to follow? How do you break them? What does this say about the way you were trained by your family? What other rules do you like to break?"

4. Optional: "What are the rules which you think are the most important? When do you experience the group at its best? What rules or agreements help support this positive experience?"

5. "Now bring yourself back into the room. Feel your feet on the floor. Take a few more breaths and rejoin the room."

6. Then each man shares the patterns which he saw in himself.

7. When each man is finished, the group can talk over what rules they want to keep and which they want to throw out. (This can be a lengthy process which takes more than one meeting.)

8. The leader closes the group in the usual way.

COMMENTS

Life is constructed with rules, taboos and conscious and unconscious agreements. Being aware of these rules, and how we create them, can help us change them. In a group a few years ago, one man was moving a lot and eating some peanuts, while we discussed the issue of "evil," what is it and how do we manifest it.

He got feedback from others in the group that he was irritating them, and finally he said, "This topic makes me really nervous. I'm sorry if I could not be more direct with you. But I have seen evil and it makes me very scared." He had been breaking a rule which our group had never articulated-that we not distract the group from the man who is speaking.

CREATING THE GROUP, REVISITED   DISCUSSION

DESCRIPTION

These exercises help men to talk about group agreements and under-standings. Agreement about these topics creates a set of benchmarks that group members can refer back to as the group continues. The discussion of such core topics creates group safety and cohesion.

STEPS

1. The leader for the night starts the group in the usual way.

2. He starts a group discussion by asking one of the following questions.

   A. What kind of group do I want to be in? (You can refer to Chapter Four and Five for possible answers.)

   B. What is my commitment to the group: time, attention, etc.? Will I make group participation a priority?

   C. What kind of leadership do I want in the group? Am I willing to be a leader? Will I be willing to deal with my issues about leadership in an honest, non-blaming way?

3. Men go around the circle and answer whichever question the group leader has recommended.

4. Open dialogue can follow after the whole group has commented on a question.

5. The leader closes the group in the usual way.

COMMENTS

I bring up these same questions again, because the group is always working with them. The discussions on this page should take two to three weeks, if each question is investigated deeply.

INTERPERSONAL DYNAMICS, REVISITED DISCUSSION

DESCRIPTION

These exercises help men to talk about personal dynamics which will emerge as the group meets. The open discussion of such core group topics creates safety and cohesion.

STEPS

1. The leader for the night starts the group in the usual way.

2. He starts a group discussion by asking one of the following questions.

   A. What is my greatest fear in this group? What might go wrong that would hurt me?

   B. What method would I use to stay isolated from the group? (Humor, sarcasm, criticism of others, spacing out, not coming.)

   C. What family patterns do I feel are evoked by my participation in the group?

   D. Who dominates the airtime in the group? What is he talking about during this time? How do the group members feel at these times? Interested, passive, angry, bored?

   E. Are men committed to truthtelling instead of blaming? Are they willing to practice being self-responsible?

3. Men go around the circle and answer whichever question the group leader has recommended.

4. Open dialogue can follow after the whole group has commented on a question.

5. The leader closes the group in the usual way.

COMMENTS

These particular activities require men to talk about the inner experience of the group, and it asks the members to be vulnerable and non-blaming. I bring up these same questions again, because the group is always working with them. These discussions should take several weeks, if each question is investigated deeply.

Connection with the Group   Creative Arts

Description
This movement exercise helps men talk about how connected they feel with the group. It creates a dialogue which develops group intimacy.

Steps:
1. The leader for the night starts the group in the usual way.

2. The leader then puts an object in the middle of a large circle which represents the group.

3. He then asks the men to arrange themselves in the room spatially in a way that describes how close they feel to the group members and to the group process. Are they engaged, interested, committed? If they feel connected, they should stand close to the center, and if they feel disconnected, they should stand at the edges of the room.

4. The men should take a few minutes to move to the place that feels the most comfortable or connected to them. It is okay to move around into different spaces, but eventually they should settle on one.

5. After each man has finished, the leader can start a discussion on these questions: What does each man feel in the different positions? What do the men in different positions want to say to each other? What would it take for the men to change positions, either move in closer to the group or move away?

6. Optional: The group can make another circle, in which each man positions himself where he wants to be in relation to the group. The same questions can be asked as in step 5, plus these: What prevents you from creating the group as you want it to be?

7. The leader closes the group in the usual way.

Comments
These patterns of closeness and distance show up in work and relationship, and often go back to family of origin issues of inclusion and exclusion. We want to blame others for the way we create these patterns. The empowerment here comes when we see our own role in the process, and take responsibility for the way we want it to be.

CHAPTER 10

STAGES IN THE GROUP'S LIFE
GOING DEEPER AGAIN

Just as groups can cycle through different levels of connection and interest, they can cycle through and repeat different activities. Activities done at the beginning of the group's life will have a very different feeling later, when the group has developed more trust. Often the simplest of activities go the deepest.

My own experience as a leader and participant is that group life can always provide more healing and teach us more about intimacy. There is no end to our human needs for love, friendship, creativity, and truth. A group is like some fantastic art process which grows in depth as I put more attention into it.

It is also with some sorrow that I realize how deep our conditioning is; healing ourselves is a life long journey through the lands of sloth and fear. But a good group of compadres can give us courage, and the goal of giving more love and creativity to the world and our families is worth a great sacrifice and a great effort.

I have brought together two types of exercises in this chapter.

1. Deeply Evocative Exercises: Some of the family drama practices which involve re-enactments of childhood wounding can bring up old, painful memories. Some groups have brought in outside facilitators to provide greater support

   Entering a Man's House
   Naked Came the Stranger
   Group Massage
   Healing Family Violence
   Writing Our Eulogy
   Oracle Wisdom

2. Complex Ritual or Creative Activities: Some activities may be hard to do in the group until members have developed a skill at leading ritual or arts activities. Some of these require the leader to lead and not participate.

   Fairy Tale Writing
   Spontaneous Poetry
   Forgiveness Meditation

All these exercises should be done later in the group's life together (at least several months), after men have built up trust, after they are familiar with expressing feelings together, and after the group has practiced rituals and complex activities.

ENTERING A MAN'S HOUSE   DISCUSSION

DESCRIPTION
Often we forget how our possessions and our home reflect our values and
affect our moods. In this exercise, group members receive feedback about
the relationship between our inner lives (our soul and character) and our
outer lives (our homes).

STEPS
0. Prior to the meeting, the group agrees to do this activity and decides
   whose house to meet at. The man who is hosting should set appro-
   priate limits about how far he feels comfortable letting the men into
   his domain.

1. The group leader starts the group in the usual way.

2. Each man in the group spends fifteen to thirty minutes going
   through the man's house: drawers, possessions, office, refrigerator,
   garage, car. He thinks about the man's possessions, about the way
   the man lives, and what he knows about the man from the group or
   any other contact.

3. The group makes a circle, and one by one, each member tells the
   man what he has learned about him, in a non-judgemental way.

4. Optional: The man tells the story of his house and his possessions
   for ten to fifteen minutes. Does he feel good about his home and his
   "stuff"? How does he feel seeing the men move through his physical domain?

5. The man responds to the group after everyone has spoken, or after
   each man has shared with him.

6. Optional: The group can end with some form of blessing and thanks
   for the man opening himself up in this way.

7. The leader ends the group in the usual way.

COMMENTS
This activity was suggested by Denis Sutro, Corte Madera, CA

NAKED CAME THE STRANGER

DISCUSSION

DESCRIPTION

This exercise allows men to release old shames and secrets about our bodies. We carry in secrecy so many judgements and beliefs about the way we look, and we constantly compare ourselves to other men.

STEPS:

1. The group leader starts the group in the usual way.

2. Then everyone in the group takes all their clothes off.

3. One man stands before the group and talks about the various strengths and weaknesses of his body. He describes how he feels about his body: its various parts and as a whole; then he describes how it is changing over time.

4. When the man is finished, the group members may ask him questions or make comments about anything they see in his presentation, posture, expression, etc.

5. Each man in the group talks about his body in this way.

6. Then the group can share together what it is like to see all these bodies. Members can talk about their comparisons between body appearances and feelings of competitiveness which might arise.

7. Optional: Take individual or group photo of naked men.

8. The group leader closes the group in the usual way.

COMMENTS

Men should agree on this activity the meeting before, since there is a tremendous taboo against group nudity. Groups can build up trust in each other by taking saunas or hot tubs together or by a massage activity. When I think about my own body, I remember all the wounds I received, from baseball spikes, kitchen knives, and sexual disasters, and all of its incredible vitality and athleticism. I keep so many of these joys and sorrows secret, not sure that anyone really wants to hear about them.

This activity was suggested by Bob Densmore, Woodacre, CA, with added ideas from Chris Harding, Dorchester, MA.

MATERIALS

A camera and film, if the group wishes to record all these male bodies.

GROUP MASSAGE   CREATIVE ARTS

DESCRIPTION
This exercise gives men the human touch that they so often forget to give themselves; often feelings and memories about abuse, parents' touching, and fear of other men will come up. We need to practice nurturing touch and receptivity.

STEPS:
1. The leader starts the group in the usual way.

2. One man lies down in the middle of the floor or on a massage table and each man helps massage him for ten or fifteen minutes.

3. Optional: As the volunteer lies in the group, the leader says to him softly, "Let yourself breathe in and receive the good wishes and affection of the group. Just relax, breathe and feel the touch of the men." The leader can repeat these statements a few times.

4. Optional: The leader can say, "Let yourself remember other men's touch, both affectionate and harmful. Just breathe into these memories and send love to them, as the men send love to you."

5. If he wants to, when the group massage is done, the man can reflect on any memories or feelings which came up for him.

6. When the first man is complete, then the next man lies down and the process continues.

7. When all the members are finished with their massages, the group is usually quite relaxed. The members can check in if they want to.

8. Then the leader closes the group in the usual way.

COMMENTS
Our lives are so busy that we forget the simple pleasures: sunrise, fresh air, the touch of a friend. This exercise lets men relax into a simple human need: affectionate touching. The group should be prepared for deep feelings being stirred up.

Men are so often criticized for lacking nurturing qualities, but I have noticed that we are capable of nurturing, if we are given permission, models, and a safe environment.

This activity was suggested by Ken Cross of San Rafael, CA.

MATERIALS
Massage table, oil, etc., if the group wants these.

HEALING FAMILY VIOLENCE   CREATIVE ARTS

DESCRIPTION

Each man gets to share deeply his feelings about a family scene from his youth which had a big impact on him. Often in the original scene, he couldn't express himself fully. During the exercise, deep truths can come out which allow the man to understand and change his own emotional patterns.

STEPS

1. The group leader starts the group in the usual way.

2. The group leader says, "Think about an important scene in your past, a scene in which emotional or physical violence was done to you. Imagine where you were and who was with you. How big were they? Remember the physical positions of all the members of the family, whether or not they were there in the scene. (For example, in a scene with your father abusing you, you can include your mother in a different part of the house. Maybe she turns her head away; she didn't want to know.) Let yourself see and feel this old scene in your memory."

3. One by one, each group member creates the family scene, using the other members of the group. He selects someone to play each of the participants in the scene, then he puts them into the scene and arranges their bodies and their expressions so that they represent what the creator of the scene remembers.

4. The group member then puts himself into the scene as the boy who went through this event.

5. He recounts to the other members what it is like to be the boy in the scene. He can express whatever he wants to the other members of the family scene. (Expressions of rage, loss or great pain can occur here. The leader should help the man share as deeply as he needs to.

6. Other members in the scene can express their feelings about being in the scene, or what they feel about the boy. Dialogue can develop between these characters.

7. When the dialogue ends, and the member feels that he has expressed whatever he wants to, that scene dissolves.

8. The group can either discuss the scene, or go on to the next man's memory.

COMMENTS

This is a very evocative exercise! It comes from Virginia Satir's work with families. The group should appoint a leader for the night who can help and encourage the full expression of the feelings. It may take a whole night for one man's drama to come to completion. This exercise can also be designed to dramatize times when each man did violence to others. Great learning about our own violent patterns can be uncovered.

WRITING OUR EULOGY   CREATIVE ARTS

DESCRIPTION
This evocative exercise helps men see who they are and who they would like to become. The presence of death is constant in our lives, but how many of us have the courage to live with this reality?

STEPS
1. The leader for the night starts the group in the usual way.

2. He then distributes pens and paper and says to the men: "Write as quickly as possible for about ten minutes. The topic is your eulogy. What would you like people to say about you? What do you imagine they will actually say."

3. Men start writing and the leader can put on some soft music if he wants to.

4. After the men write, they share their eulogies in turn. The group gives each one feedback after his writing.

5. After each man has finished, the leader can start a general discussion if he wants.

6. The leader closes the group in the usual way.

COMMENTS
One time after we did this activity, a man said, "I started to hear the eulogy at my father's funeral. It was given by a priest who didn't know him. I felt so enraged then. No one knew what a bastard he was. I'm so tired of all the secrets. No one knows me either, when I think about my isolation. Goddamn it," he shouted. "I want to live." He was standing and shaking with energy now. "I want to live. I want to express love for my kids and my wife." He started howling and dancing for life as the men in the room clapped time to his wild dance. "I want to live," he shouted over and over. Men cheered loudly, and when the man stopped several minutes later, winded and happy, one of the other men said, "Best funeral I was ever at." We all laughed untill we hurt.

MATERIALS
Pen and paper for participants.

ORACLE WISDOM   RITUAL

DESCRIPTION

A man going through a transition (death, birthday, divorce) can receive support in a deep way. Men can use this process to share knowledge from their soul or imagination. Touching these voices outside of our normal personalities and our points of view is an important part of the healing process.

STEPS

0. Prior to the meeting, the group should plan this event, since materials have to be brought, and since it takes a good deal of group time.

1. The group leader starts the group in the usual way. The man whom the group is focusing on explains the transition which he is going through.

2. The group leader then puts the pile of sticks in the middle of the room. The group sits quietly together and imagines what characteristics they want each stick to represent: humor, insight, courage, honesty, etc.

3. Each man in the group picks up a stick. At that time, each man decides on a characteristic from the list above. He will try to speak to this man from the point of view of that quality. Then the men stand randomly in the group room and form an imaginary forest, each one holding his stick.

4. The group leader then asks for a few minutes of silence so that the men can meditate on their characteristic and what they want to say to the man.

5. The man in transition wanders through the symbolic forest, and requests advice and help from each tree. The man holding that stick (honesty, courage, etc.) speaks directly to him from that point of view, and says what he thinks the man should do or be careful of. For example: I am courage. I see you taking a risk. I see you strong enough to not know what is going to happen and still going forward. You will land on your feet."

6. After the man has gone through the whole forest, the circle reconvenes and men share and talk to each other.

7. The leader ends the group in the usual way. This is a good opportunity to give a group hug to the man who went through the process.

COMMENTS
This exercise seems complicated, but it has proved to be very powerful.

MATERIALS
A bundle of sticks (one to six feet long, but uniform in length), one for each man in the group.

This activity was developed by my Thursday night group, in Mill Valley and Fairfax, CA.

Fairy Tale Writing

Creative Arts

Description
This exercise helps men to practice thinking mythologically and imaginatively; it shows us how our lives are shaped by myth.

Steps
0. Prior to meeting, members should agree to read at least one fairy tale, so that images are stirred up in their imaginations.
1. The leader for the night starts the group in the usual way.
2. The leader begins a short discussion of the fairy tales which men have read based upon the fundamental building blocks of the fairy tale listed below. In other words: what are the qualities of the main characters; what are the common locations, conflicts; and the agreements and bargains which help make a fairy tale work? (The discussion serves as preparation for the writing.)
2. Men take the handout (described below) and make quick notes next to each of the entries in the list: what kind of characters do they want in their story, what conflicts, what magic, etc.
3. After a brief period of note-taking (five to ten minutes), men write a short fairy tale in about thirty minutes.
4. Then they read their fairy tales one by one to the group.
5. The leader asks the men to answer the key question: how are the conflicts and plot in this fairy tale like your life right now? The men answer the question individually, and then the group also answers the question for each story and each man.
6. Optional: The group can end with a ritual blessing to all the archetypes and inner characters who were brought into the group.
7. The group leader ends the group in the usual way.

Comments
Men often find this writing and talking stirs up their imaginations and is very enjoyable. This activity, like other creative arts work, helps men develop their right brain, with its imagination and poetic consciousness, and its direct access to our intuition. These pathways are the 'roads less taken' in our hurry-up lives.

Materials
Pen and paper; a handout with the following words in a vertical list: Characters, plot, conflict, magic, agreement, location(s), bargains, happy ending.

SPONTANEOUS POETRY RITUAL

DESCRIPTION
Men practice using creative language, and this exercise takes us outside of our usual logical thought system. It also engenders spiritual feelings, and helps us open our vision to see our lives in a broader perspective.

STEPS
1. The group leader starts the group as usual.
2. The leader asks the group to begin gentle drumming.
3. One by one men recite poems, from memory if possible (from Rumi, Kabir, Rilke and others) as inspiration.
4. Then when a man is moved, he stands and dances and recites from his heart what the presence of life, of beauty, of energy, of god or his higher power means and feels to him. Men should focus on using images of nature.
5. After each man speaks, drumming becomes a little louder, then it quiets as the next man speaks and dances.
6. After each man has danced and said out loud his inner vision, more poems are read or recited, and the drumming comes to an end.
7. The leader ends the group in the usual way.

COMMENTS
Men have to do a little research in poetry books to find the types of spiritual poems to use at the beginning as models. The poetic modeling at the beginning is very important to set the proper mood of appreciation and inspiration.

This activity was suggested by Peter Santulli, Sausalito, CA.

MATERIALS
Drums, poetry books (if needed).

FORGIVENESS MEDITATION   RITUAL

DESCRIPTION
Inner journeys, such as this visualization, help us to open to feelings which we may be having, but which we do not pay attention to. They also help us to become more loving people.

STEPS
1. The leader for the night starts the group in the usual way.

2. He tells everyone to make themselves comfortable, either lying down or sitting up straight, and asks them to listen to his voice.

3. Slowly, he says something like this, speaking very slowly. "We all have need for forgiveness. Bring into your mind the picture of someone whom you would like to forgive. It may be for a recent injury, or it may be for something which happened long ago. Do not force the forgiveness. Try to let it grow inside your heart for them. Imagine all the stress and pressure that forced them to hurt you or to be unkind to you. See if you can't forgive the person who did the action to you. No one is asking you to forgive the injury itself. That happened, it was painful, and it was wrong. But can you find in yourself to be your best self, to forgive the person who acted blindly and unconsciously."

4. "See if you can remember a time when you may have acted in a similar way, and hurt someone. Can you now forgive yourself for your own fear, for your own anger? Try to find in your heart some forgiveness, some loving kindness for yourself. Try to see how you were trained to react the way you did, and forgive yourself for being human, for making a mistake, for hurting another."

5. "See if you can let the feeling of forgiveness grow in your own heart. Open up to the feeling of loving kindness and acceptance. Let your heart grow warm and big with the knowledge that we all need forgiveness, we all need love. All the humans who ever walked on this planet need love and kindness. See if you can't imagine love in your heart for yourself, and then let your heart swell up with love for someone close to you whom you care about. Let your heart open and let yourself feel the greatness of your love."

6. "Now let the feeling swell and wash over others, others in this room, others you may have seen today, friends, and family. Let their faces and their voices come into your consciousness and touch the feelings of connection and love which you have for them."

7. "See if you can't now open your heart to all humans, living and

dead, who just like you have sought love on this planet of great potential for love and for loss. Just breathe into your heart and open to love for people."

8. "Now begin to bring the meditation to a close. Feel your body and the weight of gravity, let go of any deep feelings which you have and let your breathing be natural and slow. When you feel ready, open your eyes and connect with the group and we can begin to talk together."

9. After a discussion, the group leader closes the group in the regular way.

COMMENTS

This meditation can be done as a group ritual. One man sits in the middle of the circle and tells the group who he wants to forgive and why. Then he either imagines the person in front of him or picks someone to role play or symbolize the one to be forgiven. The man speaks out loud, saying, I forgive you (says the person's name) for ..."

The group itself can ritualize forgiveness by having each man sit in the middle. He can go around the circle, asking forgiveness for any harm that he may have caused to the other men, one by one. He can ask the group members to share any hurts with him which he may have done consciously or unconsciously, and then ask for their forgiveness.

CHAPTER 11

MEN'S RESOURCES FOR CHANGE

1. BOOKS

FAIRY TALES AND MYTHS
King Warrior Magician Lover. Moore and Gillette. HarperCollins. New York. 1990. Many positive images of men and a sympathetic analysis of our psyches.

Iron John. Robert Bly. Harper and Row. New York. 1990. The book that came from the material that started it all. How can you miss it?

The Complete Fairy Tales of the Brothers Grimm. Jack Zipes, translation. Bantam Books. 1987. The seminal work of the Grimms, a seedbed of story lines and images.

SOCIOLOGY-HISTORY
Warrior's Journey Home: Healing Men, Healing the Planet. Jed Diamond. New Harbinger. Oakland. 1994. A book that inspires change and outlines a plan to get from here to there. This book provides a thoughtful analysis of violence and addiction, and shows how men can heal from these habits, from a pioneer in the men's movement.

Manhood in the Making. David Gilmore. Yale University Press. 1990. Another sympathetic analysis of how men are trained to be the way we are. Fascinating, slightly academic, and highly intelligent.

RITUAL

Of Water and the Spirit. Malidoma Some. Tarcher-Putnam. 1994. An African shaman with a Western education describes his life in these two worlds.

Betwixt and Between: Patterns of Masculine and Feminine Initiation. Louis Mahde, Stephen Foster, and Meredith Little, eds. Open Court Publishing. 1987. An anthology of articles and descriptions of personal and tribal initiations, with information about how to create our own.

SPIRITUAL LIFE

Healing into Life and Death. Stephen Levine. Doubleday. 1987. A road map on how to work with illness, death and loss. Many valuable guided meditations.

A Path with Heart. Jack Kornfield. Bantam. 1993. Stories, autobiographical and otherwise, by a leading western teacher of Buddhism. A man with heart has chosen inspirational stories and teachings to help us wake up to living life with attention and compassion.

POETRY

News of the Universe. Robert Bly, ed. Sierra Club Books. 1980. A seminal collection of poetry on nature, mysticism, love and death, organized around Bly's thesis that nature poetry is re-emerging as a vital force in Western poetry, after centuries of misuse and ignorance.

Rag and Bone Shop of the Heart. Robert Bly, James Hillman and Michael Meade, eds. Harper Collins. 1992. A collection of poetry loved by men who have attended workshops with these three important teachers.

RELATIONSHIP

Conscious Loving. Gay Hendricks, PhD. and Katie Hendricks, PhD. Bantam. 1990. Excellent text for understanding body-oriented healing and for practicing truthtelling and non-blaming conversations. See especially the exercises in the back of the book.

2. VIDEO

A Gathering of Men. Bill Moyers. PBS. A poignant interview with Robert Bly explaining his work with men, intercut with workshop footage of men talking with each other and Bly.

3. MEN'S CENTERS

The best place to find a listing of centers in your area is:

Menstuff: The National Men's Resource Calendar
MAS Medium Co.
Box 882
San Anselmo Ca 94960-0882
Phone: 415-453-2839; $10/yr. for this quarterly publication.

CALIFORNIA

BERKELEY
Berkeley Men's Center
2925 Shattuck Ave.
Berkeley, CA 94705
415-644-0107

MARIN COUNTY
Echo Rock Therapy Center Men's Program
45 Camino Alto
Mill Valley, CA 94941
415-388-0333
Coordinator: George Taylor

SANTA ROSA, SONOMA COUNTY
Redwood Men's Center
705 College Ave.
Santa Rosa, CA
707-575-0550

LOS ANGELES
Lost Dog Men's Council, 310-475-1069

COLORADO

BOULDER
Men's Council Project
Box 17341
Boulder, CO 80301-0431
303-444-7741

NEW YORK

NEW YORK
John Guarnaschelli
On the Common Ground
250 W. 57 St. #1527
New York, NY 10107

OREGON

PORTLAND
Portland Resource Center
503-235-3433

WASHINGTON

SEATTLE
Seattle Men's Wisdom Council
206-454-1189

4. PUBLICATIONS AND PERIODICALS

Brother to Brother. P.O. Box 1876, Nevada City, CA 95959.

Journal of Men's Studies. Box 32, Harriman, TN 37748.

Men's Center of Los Angeles Newsletter. 213-276-9598.

Seattle MEN. 602 W. Howe St., Seattle, WA 98119.

Wingspan. 846 Prospect, La Jolla, CA 92037.

*George Taylor began attending men's retreats
and events in 1984, never knowing that his own
healing path would become a professional passion.
He began leading men's groups eight years ago,
and he has created several men's support programs
in the San Francisco Bay Area.*

*George is a California-licensed Marriage, Family
and Child Counselor and he leads three ongoing
groups at the Echo Rock Therapy Center in Mill
Valley, CA. He has written extensively about group
behavior and relationship for national periodicals,
and his articles and poetry have been published in
many books. He consults nationally with group
participants and leaders about group process.*

*For information about his counseling programs
and his men's groups, call him at 415-388-0333.*